Written by the Wind

Written by the Wind

Randy Stoltmann

ORCA BOOK PUBLISHERS

First edition

Canadian Cataloguing in Publication Data
Stoltmann, Randy, 1962–
   Written by the wind

   ISBN 1-55143-003-7
   1. Wilderness areas—British Columbia.   2.
Nature conservation—British Columbia.   3.
British Columbia– Description and travel–1981–
I. Title.
QH77.C2S86 1993   917.11'3   C93-091635-2

We gratefully acknowledge the financial assistance of The Canada Council.

Cover design by Christine Toller
Photo credit – front cover inset: L. DeGroot
All photos by the author except:
   page #43 and #80 — Clinton Webb

Printed and bound in Hong Kong

Orca Book Publishers
PO Box 5626, Station B
Victoria, BC   V8R 6S4
Canada

Orca Book Publishers
Box 3028, 1574 Gulf Road
Point Roberts, WA   98281
USA

To my parents who introduced me to wild places.

What we contribute to this world must be what we believe is right.
I thank you for understanding.

ACKNOWLEDGEMENTS

Completing a work such as *Written by the Wind* is the result of the intermeshing talents of many people and the inspiration brought about by the complexity and beauty of our wilderness. To the former I can attempt to extend my thanks in words, but to the latter I can only hope that my appreciation will be expressed in the form of protection for these wild places.

To my brother Greg Stoltmann and my friends, Leo DeGroot, John Duffy, Ian Mackenzie, Clinton Webb and George Yearsley, thank you for sharing these adventures with me.

To Ken Budd, with whom I collaborated to develop the original design elements and concept, and without whose advice and expertise I may never have brought this project to publication; to Elspeth Hayter, for her invaluable assistance in refining the design and laying out the chapter mock-up and cover; to Mark Kelly for the preparation of colour prints for the mock-up; and to Trevor Jones for responding to my requests for facts and figures, thank you for giving selflessly of your time and skills, and for believing in this project.

Finally, I must extend my sincerest thanks to Bob Tyrrell and the staff of Orca Book Publishers for turning a dream into reality.

For all of you, and for others who share my love and concern for these five special places, may they remain as wild as I have seen them.

Randy Stoltmann
West Vancouver
March 1993

TABLE OF CONTENTS

WRITTEN BY THE WIND: On the Boundary Line 13

GARIBALDI: Into the Wilderness 17

MEGIN: Tidewater to Treeline 33

STEIN: High Ridge Ramblings 49

KYUQUOT: Rainforest by the Sea 67

SOUTHERN CHILCOTINS: Mountains of Autumn Gold 83

WRITTEN BY THE WIND

Wander in high meadows
or lie beneath a pine
watch the river flow
and disregard the time.

Hear the singing firs
their long and supple limbs
written by the wind
into nature's ancient hymns.

Feel the warmth of summer
or winter's icy chill
through the waters of the river
and the trees upon the hill.

Softly walk the river's course
leaving only footprints in the sand
as fleeting signatures of passing
in a lovely, living land.

SELECTED BIBLIOGRAPHY

Moore, Keith. *Coastal Watersheds: An Inventory of Watersheds in the Coastal Temperate Forests of British Columbia.* Vancouver: Earthlife Canada Foundation & Ecotrust/ Conservation International, 1991.

Roemer, Hans L., Jim Pojar and Kerry R. Joy. *Protected Old-Growth Forests in Coastal British Columbia.* Natural Areas Journal, Volume 8 (3), 1988.

Sierra Club of Western Canada/The Wilderness Society. *Ancient Rainforests at Risk, An Interim Report of the Vancouver Island Mapping Project.* Victoria: Sierra Club of Western Canada/The Wilderness Society, December, 1991.

Vold, Terje. *Wilderness in British Columbia* (draft). Victoria: Ministry of Forests, Integrated Resources Branch, 1990.

GARIBALDI: Into the Wilderness

Bowers, Dan. *Exploring Garibaldi Park, Volume 2.* Vancouver: J.J. Douglas Ltd., 1977.

Culbert, Dick. *Alpine Guide to Southwestern British Columbia.* Vancouver: Dick Culbert, 1974.

Stoltmann, Randy. *Across Garibaldi Park.* The B.C. Mountaineer, Journal of the B.C. Mountaineering Club, Volume 60, 1990.

MEGIN: Tidewater to Treeline

Stoltmann, Randy. *Tidewater to Treeline, Megin River to Buttle Lake, Strathcona Park.* The B.C. Mountaineer, Journal of the B.C. Mountaineering Club, Volume 60, 1990.

KYUQUOT: Rainforest by the Sea

Anonymous. *Unpublished technical background paper on the Power River Blowdown.* Campbell River: Ministry of Forests, Campbell River Forest District, 1991.

Young, Cameron. *Clayoquot: On the Wild Side.* Vancouver: Western Canada Wilderness Committee/Summerwild Productions, 1990.

STEIN: High Ridge Ramblings

M'Gonigle, Michael, Wendy Wickwire. *Stein: The Way of the River.* Vancouver: Talonbooks, 1988.

Parker, M.L., Benjamin Parker, Leo DeGroot. *Dendrochronological Investigations in the Stein River Valley.* Contract Report to Western Canada Wilderness Committee, 1988.

Stoltmann, Randy. *Stein Skylines.* The B.C. Mountaineer, Journal of the B.C. Mountaineering Club, Volume 61, 1992.

White, Gordon R. *Stein Valley Wilderness Guidebook.* Vancouver: Stein Wilderness Alliance, 1991.

SOUTHERN CHILCOTINS: Mountains of Autumn Gold

Kimmins, J.P. *Report to the Southern Chilcotin Mountains Wilderness Society concerning Potential Boundaries for a South Chilcotin Mountains Wilderness Park.* University of British Columbia, Faculty of Forestry, 1985.

WRITTEN BY THE WIND

ON THE BOUNDARY LINE

*W*ind. Soft and capricious, or blustery and bold, wind signals change in the wilderness. As a moving air mass, wind is silent and invisible, but interfacing with landforms, water and vegetation, it speaks in sighing, rushing, howling, whistling or shrieking tones. Like a telegraph between weather systems and the land, wind flexes creaking limbs, topples trees, rustles leaves, raises waves and hurls winter's icy sandpaper against treeline trunks. Its signature abounds, written in sand and snow patterns, icy cornices and broken, flagged and matted trees.

It is late winter 1993 and I have been a part of life on Earth for just over thirty years. I have seriously explored wilderness for just over one-third of that time. Already, returning to places where a few years ago I walked through ancient forests that had evolved undisturbed, I have found newly bulldozed roads and logging slash. By the end of my lifespan, it is likely that the only wilderness that will remain in southwestern British Columbia will be that which is either protected in parks or undesirable to the forest and mining industries. Another wind blows through the hills — a brisk wind of change writing the final chapter for many wild places.

Until recently, much of British Columbia was a wilderness landscape dominated by natural processes and inhabited by relatively small human populations that lived in harmony with the land. But with the advance of logging and mineral, oil and gas exploration — industrial activities driven beyond sustainable levels by an out-of-control world marketplace — wilderness has diminished rapidly. The provincial government's 1984 Forest and Range Analysis predicted that planned forestry development alone would reduce B.C.'s primitive lands by thirty-two percent over the next twenty years. By 1988, however, mapping showed the area of wilderness to be an alarming fifty-two percent less than in the 1984 analysis, largely as a result of mineral, oil and gas exploration. Now, in the 1990s, researchers are finding that virtually no wilderness has been protected in some of the province's distinct ecological regions, and the remaining options for doing so are rapidly disappearing.

As of 1992, parks and designated wilderness areas in B.C. amounted to approximately six percent of the provincial land base. Another fifty-six percent of the land base was roadless, but more than half of that comprised icefields, alpine, subalpine or scrub forests in the Coast Mountains and remote portions of northern B.C. Between the high ridges and plateaus, logging roads continue to push further towards the back ends of major river valleys and tributaries, carving up the last substantial tracts of rich valley-bottom forest, often ending on the boundary line of subalpine terrain or park land. Seismic lines are slashed across the north country and mineral exploration roads are punched into pristine subalpine and alpine wilderness.

Originally, I chose the trips recounted in this book because I was interested in these remote areas from a geographical and ecological perspective. It later became apparent that these areas reflected complete experiences, covering a range of elevation and vegetation zones that represent a wide cross-section of southwestern B.C.

Kyuquot Sound and the Brooks Peninsula are on the outer west coast of Vancouver Island, where the Pacific Ocean nourishes a tangled rainforest. The Megin River valley, also on western Vancouver Island, is only slightly more sheltered but equally luxuriant. Inland from the Megin, in the mountains of Strathcona Provincial Park, a profoundly maritime climate maintains lush vegetation even on steep, rocky terrain. On the mainland, in Garibaldi Provincial Park, is a classic Coast Mountains wilderness of deeply cut valleys and high, heavily glaciated peaks and ridges. The climate is still maritime, but grades to sub-maritime in the lee of the mountains, and consequently the forests are lush but not truly rainforests. In the Stein River valley and Southern Chilcotin Mountains, the transition from coastal sub-maritime climate through sub-continental to dry interior continental climate is evident in forests with extensive fire histories and in sparser vegetation such as grasslands and open parkland-type groves.

In all of these climatic and vegetation zones in southwestern B.C., areas featuring the complete elevational range of wilderness, from valley bottom to mountain top, have become rare. The few places that remain in wilderness condition face increasing pressures from industrial and commercial interests. The rainforests of the Kyuquot area are coveted by the coastal forest industry. The Megin was scheduled for logging until its recent designation as part of Strathcona Park. Parts of Strathcona Park, the Stein and Southern Chilcotins are centres of active mineral exploration; the latter two areas contain forests claimed by the interior forest industry. Garibaldi Park, dating back to 1920, has already lost areas along its periphery to commercial ski resort developments, and faces continuing pressure from this and commercial aircraft-based recreation.

The large wilderness parks of the region protect mostly alpine and subalpine areas. Only ten percent of Garibaldi Park, seven percent of Golden Ears, nineteen percent of Manning and twenty-four percent of Strathcona are covered by old-growth forests. Pacific Rim National Park Reserve, with fifty-nine percent old-growth forest, is an exception, but its small size and coastal strip configuration makes its survival as an intact wilderness ecosystem questionable. Most low-elevation areas that are protected in these parks are geographically isolated, narrow valleys between mountain ridges, or patches and strips, like Pacific Rim, surrounded by clearcut

logging. Their genetic diversity and species composition will only decline with increased isolation.

Untouched valleys below three hundred metres in elevation are rare in these parks — only the Pitt River in Garibaldi, Moyeha and Megin rivers in Strathcona, and the Hobiton/Tsusiat system in Pacific Rim qualify. Even more rare than low valleys are low-elevation wilderness lakes. When logging began at Glacier Lake along the eastern boundary of Garibaldi Park in the early 1980s, we lost our last major low-elevation wilderness lake in the lower mainland. There are now no such wilderness lakes left; all have roads and clearcuts along their shores.

Vancouver Island provides a telling example of the state of future conservation options. Of its ninety primary river drainages over five thousand hectares in size, six remain less than two percent developed, and only two of these — the Moyeha and, more recently, the Megin — have been protected in parks. Recent mapping of Vancouver Island forests by the Sierra Club of Western Canada and The Wilderness Society shows that half the island's ancient forests that existed in 1954 had been clearcut logged by 1990. On the southern part of Vancouver Island, seventy-five percent of these forests were cut in the same thirty-six year period.

The demise of this low-elevation wilderness is cause for concern when you learn that the optimum habitat for many species of wildlife is in the low elevation forests, particularly on valley bottoms and in riparian zones along river banks and lake shores. These are the most biologically rich and diverse ecosystems, yet there is little protected. Quite literally, the majority of the parks are just "icing on the cake," while the rich body beneath is being exploited to the point of impoverishment.

Along with the wilderness itself will disappear the opportunity for exploration and discovery — to experience the overwhelming sense of mystery that the very presence of large tracts of primitive country embodies. In an age when each new hectare of park proposed must be subjected to exhaustive studies and economic analysis, its resources catalogued, quantified and mapped, it is important to remember that such all-encompassing knowledge is actually the antithesis of wilderness.

Wilderness is full of unknowns, of mystery. It is the last remnants of that "uncharted" terrain of pioneer days: one more fog-shrouded coastal canyon, one more mountain meadow home of grizzly bears that aren't wearing radio collars. Wilderness should not be defined by political boundaries and regulations, but by the ability of the land to maintain its natural functions and sustain healthy populations of native wildlife species without human manipulation. And wilderness is not just land deemed useless for other economic or social purposes, for it exists independent of these purposes as part of the original life-sustaining biosphere on which the stresses of excessive human uses have been imposed.

The following pages recount explorations of five of my favourite wilderness areas in southwestern B.C. In these places simple struggles against the timeless rhythms of nature, largely unaided by technology, remind one of the balance that exists in the natural world. Far from the trappings of civilization, one's sense of superiority quickly evaporates. In these places man is merely one creature among many. Nature becomes something to be respected, not conquered.

As I write this, new studies are being initiated under the Protected Areas Strategy and the Commission on Resources and the Environment that will affect the future of the Kyuquot, Stein and Southern Chilcotin wilderness areas. This book was created because I wish to share my experiences, insights, understanding and love of wilderness with others in an effort to promote a greater understanding of its unquantifiable value. The words are my own, but the ever-unfolding stories were written by the wind — an invitation to you to help ensure that this heritage endures.

$\mathcal{G}$ARIBALDI

INTO THE WILDERNESS

$\boldsymbol{B}$eneath my boots there is little give in the snow, still unsoftened by the morning sun. Firmly placing my ice axe and pressuring the edges of my boot soles to gain purchase, I traverse carefully, aiming for the line of sunlight creeping steadily across the surface of Macbeth Glacier. Once in the sun, where the warmth draws sweat from my forehead and beneath my backpack, the snow is soft enough to kick deep, bucket-like steps in. The ascent to the divide goes quickly with the anticipation of seeing new country beyond. From the crest, a 2,250-metre-high saddle between Couloir Ridge and

Mount Iago, my brother Greg and I gaze eastward into the untrodden wilderness beyond the Spearhead Range. No signs of human presence mar the vista: no logging cuts, no roads, no huts, no trails, no aircraft — just valleys and mountains and glaciers, a landscape shaped only by the forces of nature.

Wilderness. For the next week, this is the world in which we will live — the land as it has been for centuries. It will not always be easy nor entirely pleasant, but it will be rewarding. We heft our packs and start off down Iago Glacier.

Our trek had begun the previous day, Au-

Evening at camp one, Macbeth Glacier

gust 1. Along with two friends, we drove from Whistler and hiked to Singing Pass, then traversed below Overlord Glacier and across the boulder-strewn Fitzsimmons Glacier. Beside Overlord Glacier we watched eleven mountain goats, some of them kids, scale with astounding ease the crumbling, reddish rock on the north face of Fissile Peak, while we stumbled down a loose moraine — a ridge of gravel and boulders left when the glacial ice retreated.

That night the four of us camped by a small pool on the rim of another steep moraine separating Macbeth and Fitzsimmons glaciers. The evening was calm; rosy light descended on the peaks and the valley below lost its colours to even shades of blue. Rolls of cloud, painted by the declining sun, hung above mounts Decker and Trorey. When our friends returned to Singing Pass the following morning, Greg and I turned east into the wilderness.

Our planned route would traverse the seldom-visited heart of Garibaldi Provincial Park, south and west through river valleys and high passes, eventually ending at Diamond Head — a distance of approximately ninety kilometres. Our packs, loaded with ten days' food supply, tent, stove, fuel, extra clothing, emergency gear and ice axes, weighed in at about twenty-seven kilograms each.

Greg and I have done countless hikes and ski trips together, but this was to be our first week-long trek through trail-less mountains.

Two years younger and perhaps a little bolder, I'm the one who tends to come up with trip ideas, so am usually the planner and navigator. Greg follows along, unphased by physical difficulties — quiet, strong and stubborn enough to force passage through the densest bush. In many ways we're both loners, more thinkers than talkers, but our long relationship has developed a common sense of purpose evident in the simple, unspoken coordination of tasks that we both know need to be done to complete a journey.

UPPER CHEAKAMUS

I'm aware that the descent from the saddle down the east side of the Spearhead Range represents not only our physical entry into the wilderness, but also our psychological entry, for behind the mountain barrier we lose touch with the visual connections to civilization — distant roads, logging cuts, ski resorts and lights — that are symbols of people and services we come to rely on in everyday life. At first a little unsettling, the departure soon brings a growing emotional connection to the land and an unhindered attention to the details of natural cycles and the ongoing, simple processes of living and travelling efficiently and safely in the wild. Here our actions are governed by self-reliance.

The descent of Iago Glacier is a quick glissade — a mountaineer's form of boot skiing — down the soft snow at its edge. Twenty minutes later we are hiking along the shore of a lake not shown on the map — a milky green, iceberg-studded pool recently uncovered by the retreating glacier. Two hundred and fifty metres below we reach the willow-covered flats bordering Diavolo Creek, where streams from several glaciers merge and flow off towards the Cheakamus River. Here clumps of crimson Indian paintbrush bloom throughout the valley. Pausing in the warm sun, I crouch low to photograph the flowers framing the tortured ice of Diavolo Glacier to the west.

Downstream, where Diavolo Creek turns south and enters a small canyon, Greg and I

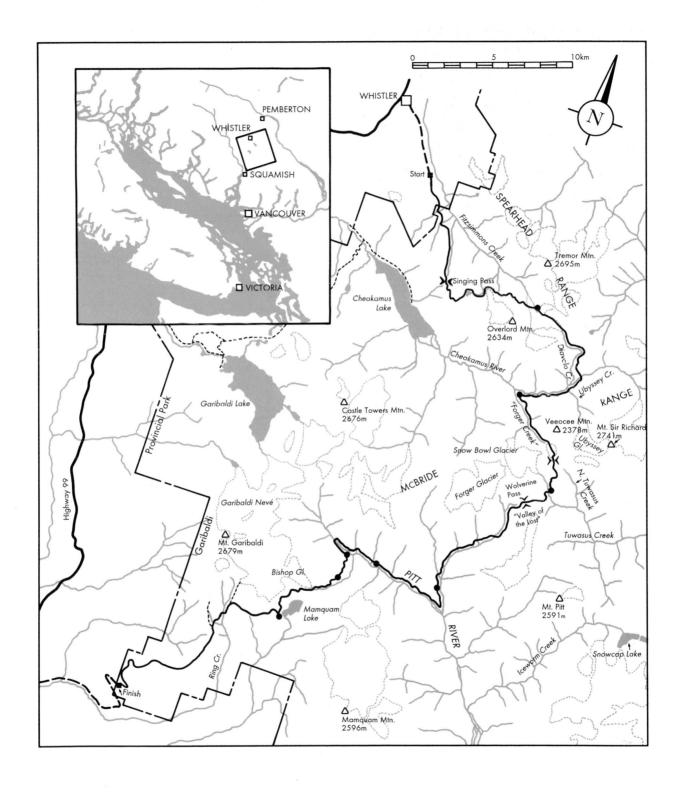

WHISTLER

PEMBERTON

WHISTLER

SQUAMISH

VANCOUVER

VICTORIA

Start

SPEARHEAD

Fitzsimmons Creek

Singing Pass

Tremor Mtn.
2695m

RANGE

Cheakamus
Lake

Overlord Mtn.
2634m

Diavolo Cr.

Cheakamus River

Ubyssey Cr.

RANGE

Garibaldi Lake

Castle Towers Mtn.
2676m

"Forget Creek"

Veeocee Mtn.
2378m

Mt. Sir Richard
2741m

Ubyssey
Gl.

Provincial Park

Snow Bowl Glacier

MCBRIDE

Forger Glacier

Wolverine
Pass

N. Tuwasus
Creek

Highway 99

Garibaldi Nevé

"Valley of
the Lost"

Tuwasus Creek

Garibaldi

Mt. Garibaldi
2679m

Bishop Gl.

PITT

Mamquam
Lake

Mt. Pitt
2591m

Ring Cr.

RIVER

Iceworm Creek

Snowcap Lake

Finish

Mamquam Mtn.
2596m

Indian paintbrush, Diavolo Glacier moraine

pause to study the aerial photos. These clearly show vegetation and terrain features — a valuable addition to the 1:50,000-scale topographical maps we normally carry. We decide to bypass the canyon by climbing over a low, treed ridge to a series of meadows east of the creek. Scattered clumps of mountain hemlock and subalpine fir soon open up to a small willow-lined creek valley. A chain of pretty meadows leads south towards the Cheakamus River. Fresh deer tracks form distinct trails in the wet soil, but the animals remain elusive. Then the forest begins to thicken, and the roar of the Cheakamus River becomes more pronounced. Descending quickly through steep, open forest, we are soon on the forested flats bordering the river where a fresh breeze blows down off the glaciers.

Downstream, wedged among boulders, a log spans the channel, here more a creek than a river. The crossing puts us right into a tangle of slide alder bushes and poison-spined devil's club on the opposite bank. I can already hear Greg cursing as he thrashes through the tangled stems. After a few minutes of difficult travel, tall trees shade out the brush and for an hour we traverse steep sidehill forests while the river below descends into a canyon.

Near a patch of pleasant open forest, the rushing of Ubyssey Creek becomes audible as it cascades down from the glaciers of 2,741-metre Mount Sir Richard. Ubyssey Creek was named by members of the University of B.C.'s Varsity Outdoors Club, who first climbed many of the peaks here in the late sixties and early seventies.

We remove our boots and wade the creek's icy waters, then sit down on the warm rocks to dry our feet while we have lunch. The drone of an airplane briefly intrudes on our primitive world, but its noise is soon lost behind the mountains, leaving us engulfed in the natural sounds and rhythms of water and wind.

Beyond Ubyssey Creek we scramble up a steep bank onto the sidehill. In the forest we are attacked by swarms of aggressive mosquitos with their annoying whining, tickling and pin-prick stings. An hour downstream we reach a flat beside the Cheakamus River where a major avalanche chute comes down off Veeocee Mountain. A slide must have really hammered down here, for even the resilient slide alder bushes are flattened, broken and dead. This makes walking easier, but the good fortune doesn't last long; away from the centre of the swath the bush is alive, flexible and tangled.

One does not walk through slide alder as much as one climbs and crawls over and under it. The downward flow of avalanches and creep of winter snow bends the dense clusters of flexible

Cheakamus River near Ubyssey Creek

trunks downhill, usually across the direction of travel up or down a valley. The ice axes on our packs catch on every overhead stem and act like well-designed anchors.

A foaming white creek storms down the chute, forming a waterfall as it breaches a cliff on the valley side. On the valley floor the stream spreads out and flows among the slide alder, which make a springy and unpredictable bridge. We negotiate the creek and cross a marsh on downed trees, finally re-entering the forest after a half-hour of damp and bushy hiking.

Tall Engelmann spruce line the river. The forest floor is covered by sand and gravel deposits, the result of flooding during spring runoff. Just downstream, where the flat valley bottom ends, the river enters another canyon. On the steep side-hills above, the forest remains very open. Animal trails are abundant and distinct, although not usually continuous enough to be followed for long. These primitive paths climb over logs and tunnel under brush thickets, making them awkward for humans to use. Rounding a ridge to the south, we encounter another large avalanche path thickly overgrown with devil's club and slide alder. Fortunately, the slides have missed a narrow strip of evergreen forest along the edge of the deep gorge. Here we find easier walking and views of the river boiling far below, its heavy booming echoing up off the rock walls.

Beyond the avalanche chute the forest is beautiful. Large old hemlocks with richly furrowed bark block out the sun, creating a sensation of primordial dimness. The air is cool, still and damp, permeated with the mustiness of decaying wood. Thick moss, spongy underfoot, carpets the forest floor, flowing over ridges and hummocks, outlining the shapes of centuries-old stumps and windfalls. After an hour's easy walking, we emerge from the ancient grove near a stream we call "Forger Creek." The open gravel bars along the Cheakamus are bathed in low-angle afternoon sunlight; the river sparkles and the air is warm. Craggy Douglas-firs — for me classic signatures of the wilderness — clothe the opposite bank.

Bear tracks, upper Cheakamus River

Glancing at the sand, I see footprints. Bear tracks. Black bear. Greg is already busy pulling gear from his pack, for this is unquestionably a wonderful place to camp. He starts setting up the tent, while I rig a rope to a leaning snag to hang up the food. Standing back and viewing my food cache, I can see that most bears would have no trouble getting at it — an adult black bear can reach three metres off the ground and the pack hangs barely two metres up. I shinny up the snag again and rig the rope higher. In these dense coastal forests, large mammals often remain elusive, but the knowledge that they still roam free and unmolested, uncounted and mysterious, adds to the special aura of wilderness.

We cook soup on the gas stove, then attempt, and fail miserably, to fry pancakes in a dented, sticky aluminum pan. A small fire in a deep pit in the sand prolongs the evening. The muffled roar of the river and the wide, clear sky above is soothing. And there is the feeling of intense satisfaction that comes with the anticipation of many wilderness days and nights ahead.

THE HEART

In the morning we pack up and eliminate the fire pit and all signs of our camp. Sometimes, for the fun of it, I make imitation deer tracks in the sand with two forefingers. It seems only natural to leave a special place just as you found it,

Seldom-climbed Mount Pitt

passing gently over the land and leaving behind only footprints — just another animal track.

We now leave the Cheakamus and start up Forger Creek, soon encountering thickets of young trees in an old glacial moraine area. Guided by the aerial photo, which shows possible weaknesses in the barrier, we traverse slide alder tangles and subalpine fir groves, working our way up to the crest of the old moraine, then follow its spine until cliffs force us to descend. The entire slope of the moraine down to Forger Creek is covered in dense, young slide alder. Half bum-sliding, shielding our eyes from twigs, we descend through the thickets to the boulder-strewn gravel wash along the creek.

The rocky valley is easy walking, with the steep Snow Bowl Glacier icefall looming above to the west. Some of these glaciers are remark-

able, having retreated several kilometres over the last sixty years, exposing large areas of barren boulder moraines. It's fascinating to think that in the 1920s much of the area where we struggled through bush this morning was under forty or fifty metres of ice.

After scrambling up another high, loose moraine into the upper valley, and ascending past the small glacier at its head, Greg and I reach Wolverine Pass — the 1,905-metre divide separating the Cheakamus drainage from that of Tuwasus Creek, a tributary of the Lillooet River.

From Wolverine Pass, near the geographic centre of Garibaldi Park, we look south to the wild country surrounding the upper Pitt River. The twin blades of remote Mount Pitt, flanked by blue-crevassed Solitude Glacier, stand in the centre of our view. Pitt's 2,591-metre summit was first climbed in 1938 by two brothers in an epic journey from the railway station at Garibaldi. Following the first ascent, the peak was climbed only twice over the next forty years, both times by parties flown in to Snowcap Lake a few kilometres to the southeast. I feel that the use of aircraft has become all to common in modern mountaineering, to the point where it is employed more for convenience than out of necessity. It seems odd that those who seek the challenge of ascending a seldom-climbed peak use modern technology to avoid the very challenge of remoteness.

To the right is an unnamed, and unclimbed, double summit. The cleft of North Tuwasus Creek, streaked with alder-choked avalanche swaths, joins the forested valley of Tuwasus Creek which leads east, out of view, towards the Lillooet River.

Dropping to a notch in the divide, we traverse southwest across a snowfield to the meadowed crest of a ridge overlooking a hanging valley. As is so often the case in this country, we are surrounded by the continuous roar of water from the many streams cascading down from the hanging icefields. Greg finds a meltwater trickle, and we settle down for lunch while taking in a panorama of mountains and valleys that few people have seen. If the heavily trodden western fringes of Garibaldi Park — Diamond Head, Garibaldi Lake, Black Tusk, Singing Pass — are its public face, then these places hidden deep within the living, breathing wilderness body surely must be its heart.

It seems strange that such a rarely visited area lies so close to Vancouver. But it is precisely this unknown aspect that harbours the spirit of wilderness; even the easy access of trails would diminish the sense of remoteness that exists here. And humans have never been very successful at reversing the effects of their developments; they work at expanding and improving until the original quality is sharply diminished. There was a time when I thought that perhaps the trail system should be expanded to relieve pressure on popular areas and provide access to remote valleys and passes. But now, having felt the wildness, I hope that this land will always remain as I have experienced it — totally wild for those who venture beyond the commonplace, in search of the heart and spirit.

Only a few wispy clouds are scudding over Mount Pitt. Earlier, I had noticed a tiny lake on the topographical map and thought it might make a pleasant campsite. The shimmering pool is now visible at 1,325 metres near treeline below the hanging valley to the west.

We sling our heavy packs onto our shoulders again and start down the steep meadow slopes into the hanging valley. The slope is covered with slick grass and heather, so we unstrap our ice axes and use them to guard against slips. Kicking my boots into marmot and pika burrows for footholds, and thrusting the pick of my axe into sod and heather clumps, I work my way across the slope above a cliff band covered with a dense mat of stunted subalpine fir and yellow-cedar. Grabbing a handful of yellow-cedar branches, I lower myself down a gully which leads to the meadow below. Greg follows and we quickly walk down to a meadowed bench still some distance above the creek. Pushing through a hemlock thicket to the final meadow slopes, our cautious walking becomes looser and more rapid as we near the valley floor. At the bottom, the cold creek offers a welcome drink.

The little lake still seems some distance

Sunset over the Spearhead Range

Ptarmigan

away, so we waste no time starting down the creek bank, soon entering dense tangles of yellow-cedar and mountain hemlock matted and distorted by winter avalanches. The creek plunges noisily over huge rocks, then suddenly leaps over a cliff, twisting some fifty metres into an alder-choked gully. I can see no way down on this side, so we cross the creek and crash through the bush to the edge of the cliff.

But the prospects here are no better. We could climb the cliff, but would face a tangled mess of slide alder at the bottom. As it is almost eight o'clock, we decide to head back up to the meadow and face this horror in the morning.

A half-hour later in camp, eating in the darkness, defeated by the bush and cliffs, my impression is of a dismal little valley. The creek roars on into the night as I lie in my bag and think about our progress. Three days, thirty-four kilometres. I feel a curiously positive stress that I haven't experienced before, like an acknowledgement of the unknown challenges ahead: how much more bush will slow our progress? Will the thin blue lines of creeks on the map become unfordable torrents? Time? Weather?

But it is these unknowns that fuel the sense of adventure. Each trip is a progression of feelings. The initial apprehension brought about by unknown terrain, remoteness and bad weather fades into an acceptance of nature's rhythms, a process of becoming part of the flow of life on the land. By the trip's end, the inevitability of leaving the elegant simplicity of wilderness becomes disappointing. Sometimes the pace slows in an effort to prolong the return to lives dominated by controlled time, rules and a false sense of urgency not connected to natural needs and cycles.

VALLEY OF THE LOST

This morning, August 4, it is cool and partly cloudy, but the sun pokes through down Tuwasus Creek, then creeps up to our camp. Breaking camp quickly, and armed with long pants, we start up a rock slide, following narrow corridors of bush-free boulders which I noticed on the aerial photo over breakfast. Carefully tracing our route on the photo, we emerge just below the gap that is our passage west towards the Pitt River. We've avoided the cliffs and bush!

We scramble up a talus slope of loose rocks to the gap which Greg has named "Valley of the Lost." There is something fitting about this, for the bleak pass evokes a powerful feeling of remoteness. Tuwasus Creek valley to the east is now hidden. To the north and south are high walls of greyish rock, and fog-shrouded peaks above. To the west, the valley curves below hanging glaciers and disappears into an unnamed canyon. In all directions it is several days' travel through difficult mountain country to the nearest road or convenience. I have often looked into the wilderness from the fringes, but here I am in the middle of it and it feels different. The time and physical energy we have invested in reaching this pass and our gradual entry into the natural cycle seem to have manifested themselves in a deeper and purer appreciation of our place in the wild. This is something precious but very fragile, something easily broken by human technology, such as aircraft which shrink the scales of time and distance that are the very measures of remoteness.

A permanent snowfield fills the Valley of the Lost despite its modest elevation of just over 1,400 metres. On the edge of the snow

View west from Wolverine Pass towards Mamquam Mountain

lies a deep green pool bordered by the steep rock walls. We walk across the snow towards the meadows beyond, rounding a damp sedge flat and climbing around a heather-covered ridge. A pretty little stream coursing through the meadows is joined by another from the north branch of the valley. Together they flow off towards the Pitt River to the southwest.

An hour through rolling meadows, willow thickets and talus slopes, where boulders have cascaded down from gullies above, brings us to within a few metres of the creek. I spot what looks like a safe place to cross just downstream where the stream flows over a granite slab. We crash down to the water's edge and replace boots with running shoes. Bare feet would be fine without a load, but the added weight of our twenty-five kilogram packs makes walking on slip-pery stones painful and hazardous. The water is cold and knee deep, but with the ice axe for balance the crossing isn't difficult. Resting on the warm rock slab while our feet dry, we study the air photos again — a major slide alder thrash lies ahead as we begin our descent into the lowlands.

The sun is out again, shining warmly as we enter the bush, heading as straight as possible towards a narrow strip of firs. Climbing through head-high salmonberry, we scramble up to the trees. Five minutes later, through the branches I can see a huge slide alder swath just ahead. I duck low and begin to negotiate the maze of flattened trunks. Over, under, over. Feeling the resistance of the branches scraping across my shoulders and pack, catching and showering bits of dried leaves and twigs on my sweaty body. More cursing and crazed enthusiasm, thrusting aside the bushes with spirited sweeps of my arms. In the midst of the slide path, a major creek storms down a rocky gully. Off with the boots and into the water, firmly gripping my ice axe, probing and balancing. The axe clangs on slick boulders, invisible under the milky glacial water. My feet slither around, looking for good footing, and I'm aware of the waterfall a few metres below. Steep, hard packed rubble on the bank is not much better, offering only marginal footing. For the moment, we are reduced to purely utilitarian travel, with the only immediate reward being that whatever we walk through ends up behind us.

From a small clearing in the alders, I spot a high waterfall foaming white over the cliffs some distance down the opposite side of the val-

Unnamed falls, upper Pitt River

ley. On our side is a huge rock slide where the entire mountainside just peeled away in one great slab and crumbled on the flats below. Some of the boulders are the size of small houses, but the natural maze is easy walking compared to the bush.

Twenty minutes later we enter the old-growth forest. After the last two hours of slide alder thrashing, it is a relief to find good travel in the forest of hemlock, amabilis fir and yellow-cedar. Across the valley, the white plume of the falls sprays down a two-hundred-metre-high slab of silver granite, vaporizing on the sharp-edged rocks below. I stop only briefly to photograph it from an opening in the forest. We want to reach the Pitt River by tonight.

Although the map names the smaller northern tributary as the Pitt River, I consider the main stem of the river to be the one which flows from the Garibaldi Nevé, an icefield to the west. The northern tributary, originating near Drop Pass, is what I call the "North Fork." The creek we are following joins the North Fork a few kilometres downstream, and we will have to cross one of the two to continue our planned route. Whether that will be possible has been a question in my mind for most of the day — at times I felt as if we might be hiking down into a trap, the only escape from which would be a long climb back up.

An hour beyond the waterfall, we descend through a grove of ancient yellow-cedars — spiral-twisted giants with flared bases clutching the mountainside, sheathed in silvery bark formed into shaggy furrows. On the valley floor we are relieved to find that what looked like more slide alder in the aerial photos is actually head-high bracken — tall but delicate ferns which part easily. Where the creek flattens out and divides around an island, we stop to gauge its depth and refill our water bottles. The question is whether to cross here or hope to find a better spot further down. Below the confluence with the North Fork, the combined creeks would be impossible to wade. Since we must eventually cross to the west side, it has become apparent that our only option short of a long detour is to cross the North Fork above the confluence.

The North Fork is a big, booming stream, larger than we had anticipated. Flowing deep and rapidly among large rocks, it looks like trouble. We say little, fully aware that we must cross it or turn back and find another route. I ponder the thundering whitewater from within the forest while Greg searches for a sturdy pole. For the first time on the trip, I seal my camera gear inside ziplock bags.

There is an island here splitting the creek into two channels, so this is probably the best crossing. The first channel is thigh deep but not very fast, so the island is easily reached. At the top end the main channel flows through a narrow gap between boulders, perhaps three metres wide, but it is very deep and fast. Too deep to wade. We wander down the island looking for a better spot, but there is none. So I pick up a log and drag it up to the gap. Greg brings another one and together we throw them across to form an unstable bridge. With a long pole upstream for balance, I inch my way across, feeling the cool tingle of water vapour on my face and arms.

Once across the logs, I step into a frigid, metre-deep eddy and struggle against the current to the sandbar on the west bank. Greg is more tentative and slips, straddling the logs, straining to keep from being washed downstream. I immediately jump back into the water, rushing out across the eddy to grab his arm. Soon we are both safely on the sandbar. Relieved, we slosh across the sand in our cold runners, walk up the bank and sit down in a dense grove of trees for a welcome rest and some food. I am no longer convinced of our ability to make the Pitt tonight.

Sitting on a log with a handful of trail mix, I watch the lumbering cinnamon-coloured bear casually saunter down a tree that leans out over the water. He turns his big rounded head and casts a nonchalant glance towards us, then ambles off the other way, fat rump wobbling like Jell-o under shiny, rippling fur. I did not get a good enough

Indian paintbrush and lupine

look to be sure, but the colour and form suggests a small grizzly. I wonder if that bear has ever seen a human before, or what he thought of our river crossing spectacle which he was obviously watching from his treetop perch.

In fading light we set off into the bush behind the little grove, shouting "Hey, bruin!," making loud "hoo hooo!" sounds and whistling. The alder gives way to an open talus slope of huge boulders. The river runs white and fast below, filling the narrow valley with its thunder. I am absorbed by a particular quality, symbolic of classic Coast Mountains lowlands, that is emitted by the blend of turbulent blue-green and white water, dim, grey cliffs and rocks swathed in exuberant vegetation, and precipitous mountainsides streaked with avalanche chutes as if someone had dragged a giant comb down their ragged, ancient forest sides.

In the midst of the canyon is a remarkable boulder, so large that it is clearly visible on the 1:70,000 scale aerial photos, perhaps forty metres long and a third as wide and high. The lower end rests on another house-sized rock which overhangs the forest edge.

Salmonberry, elderberry and slide alder close in on the talus once again, and we are returned to the clumsy, thrashing mode of travel. With this slow going, it is obvious that we cannot make the Pitt River tonight. We find a decent campsite on a mossy, flat area just at

Mount Pitt (left) and the headwaters of North Tuwasus Creek

the start of the next canyon.

While Greg cooks dinner, I string the food cache rope over the branch of a big leaning hemlock above camp, mindful of the bear in the area. The big lowland trees — several cedars and a huge hemlock beside the river, its branches draped in moss — are symbols that, at just over six-hundred metres, we have entered the coastal western hemlock zone, the wettest vegetation zone in the Coast Mountains. The roar of the river is loud, and having heard the rushing of water almost continuously for the past four days, I long for silence. But like the shuffling midnight train, it lulls me to sleep nonetheless.

THE PITT

Morning brings us a challenge: how to bypass the canyon ahead. Near the water, vertical rock walls quickly close in, and above are five-hundred metres of steep bluffs. I backtrack a short distance and push up a small clearing filled with devil's club to where I find what appears to be a long-established game trail which leads up a ledge in the bluffs. Perhaps the bear used it last night. We follow the path up around the ridge to where it fades out among the rocks. The animals have shown us the way out of the canyon. And apparently someone else as well — a red survey tape hangs from a branch. I pull it off and stuff it into the pocket of my tattered wool pants, an unnecessary sign of human presence in this primitive country. As we walk out onto an open bluff, there is a view of the Pitt River valley — all wilderness, unmarred by the roads and clearcuts that spoil so many of the low elevation valleys in the Coast Mountains. The comforting thought that this valley has been spared for its natural values relaxes me.

We make fast progress down the huge staircase of bluffs that leads to the flats bordering the Pitt. The big cedars appear again, then hemlock, amabilis fir and cottonwood beside the river. We push through the damp, fragrant bush past a slough to the river's edge. The cold silt-laden water flows fast and deep among rocks and gravel bars. Even if the first channel was fordable, I am certain the main one will be too deep and powerful to cross. Nor could we cross the North Fork where it joins downstream. Nor Iceworm Creek and one or two other major tributaries. We had considered following the Pitt downstream to the park boundary, then traversing around the south side of Mamquam Mountain to Mamquam Lake. But it is clear now that even if we could cross the river, we would be hard pressed to make it through in our five remaining days, especially with all the uncertainties. There is always the pressure to keep moving when unknown country lies ahead. A whole day could easily be squandered in the face of an unfordable river.

After a close look at the aerial photos, we decide that we must change our plans. The only viable option seems to be to follow the Pitt upstream to the Bishop Glacier tributary, then go up a hanging valley, back to the Mamquam Lake trail. The disadvantage of this route is that the air photos show heavy forest for only about two kilometres, then mostly huge alder-filled avalanche swaths and narrow forest strips all the way to the headwaters.

SLIDE ALDER HELL

We start up the sand and gravel bars, passing through a pleasant stand of young trees. Now we penetrate the big cedar forest again, hiking slowly over the uneven ground, hampered by low-hanging vine maples. An incredible crop of huge blueberries is fair compensation though.

Several hours later we reach a narrow but very bushy slide path. Beyond, we pick up an animal trail and follow it down a steep bank to a pair of creeks. Here on the banks of the Pitt, we sit on the warm rocks and eat lunch. Continuous slide alder covers the opposite side of the valley, hundreds of hectares of nearly impenetrable bush, twisted, tangled, bent and battered by avalanches, but still alive and springy. Slide alder hell!

Though we curse the way they hamper our progress, there is a sense of appreciation for the adaptation of this vegetation. Avalanches bowl over any erect trees, but the alders merely bend with the flow, often surviving under tons of cement-like snow following spring avalanches. As the snow melts, sometimes only in late summer, the alders pop up one by one, seemingly rising from their graves.

An hour after lunch we are forced uphill to avoid the first slide alder patch on our side of the river. The steep mountainside and thick undergrowth make walking tedious, fatiguing our ankles which strain against the sidehill, but it is still faster than going through the alder. After crossing a couple of narrow avalanche chutes and a creek gully thick with devil's club, we find a remarkably open patch of forest — an isolated grove of slender amabilis firs somehow missed by the slides, with a forest floor free of underbrush and strewn with twigs and bits of lichen. It is like the last refuge for evergreen trees in the midst of the slide alder kingdom.

I move forward into the next thicket — "the big swath" — a five-hundred-metre-wide slide path choked with alder, head-high salmonberry, elderberry and bracken ferns, all concealing a maze of hidden boulders and holes underneath. Every step is unpredictable, a simultaneous balancing act of pushing down and forcing up the stubborn alder trunks to allow passage. Frequently I lunge forward or teeter backwards, reacting to momentary losses of balance brought about by the pack being snagged on, or pushed by, a spring-loaded stem. My hands lash out, grasping whatever is available to restore balance, feeling the prick and sting of devil's club and salmonberry thorns. Underfoot, the latticework of branches twists and settles and sways, and I trip and stumble among boulders like a drunken idiot, cursing, swearing and sweating in the stagnant heat.

At one point I stand up on a rock and glance back, seeing a clump of wildly swaying bushes in the midst of the sea of green. Then Greg's head pops up — wearing a look of grim determination which, upon seeing me, breaks into a weak smile — as if surfacing for a gulp of air. For an hour we forge on through the green jungle, engulfed in the pungent, heady odour of crushed elderberry bushes. Finally, beyond an open creek, we are able to briefly follow the river bank, then find an escape route up a steep, eroding escarpment into a patch of forest.

Pausing for a moment while Greg catches up, I reflect on our isolation. Having been underway for nearly a week, we are mentally and physically distanced from civilization, well in

Slide alder forever . . . upper Pitt River

Hoary marmot

tune with our surroundings. In this valley, however, the sheer inefficiency of our travel and the degree of physical effort required to make headway increases our effective remoteness several-fold. The bush has set the limits, reducing travel to its slowest, most basic form, and travel time has become a more significant measure of remoteness than distance. And like the icefalls and cliffs of the peaks that are challenges on the way to achievement of the summit goal, our lowland struggle is among the purest of challenges, to be faced and overcome through simple persistence and ingenuity. Without this experience, we may miss a vital part of what wilderness is — an environment fine-tuned to its own maintenance and survival, not our convenience.

A faint animal trail briefly allows easy walking through aesthetic open forest, but all too soon ends, dropping us down the escarpment into yet another pack-snagging bush thicket. Fortunately, most of the tangled slide alder and prickly devil's club here can be bypassed by walking on the riverbank.

Clouds have been building again, and to the west, upstream, they are dark and forbidding. A few heavy rain drops begin to fall sparsely as we enter the next forest patch. There doesn't appear to be any decent campsite here near water; the river is down a steep bank. Plodding on through the gloomy forest, the light of the next swath begins to show through, but now the rain increases.

We drop down the slope to a little fir grove next to the river flats. In this secluded nook between the trees and a large rock, we set up a cozy camp and cook dinner by the tent door. What a place for a rainstorm! Right in the middle of the worst bushwhacking of the trip! It is raining hard now; the big drops are driven through the heavy forest canopy, drumming noisily on the tent tarp, merging with the river noise. It is good to know that ten hours of the most severe bushwhacking are behind us, but many hours of the same may still lie ahead.

THE CROSSING

The roar is still here early in the morning, but I cannot distinguish rain from river in my semi-conscious state. It seems dark above. Greg and I lie in our sleeping bags debating the sound in muffled grunts. I finally manage to poke my head out the tent door, and looking up can see the sky above. To my surprise all I see is blue!

The constant drinking of silty glacial water over the last two days has upset my stomach, and I feel a lack of energy and little desire to eat breakfast. I force down some oatmeal, knowing that it will be another hard day.

Starting out, we are quickly immersed in rain-soaked bush down by the river, cool wetness soaking through our clothing. The wetness also intensifies the heady aroma of the elderberries, tall, pithy-stemmed bushes that drench us with showers as we push through them. Plodding on slowly, we cross the swath and enter evergreen forest thick with much bush and windfall. With all the crisscrossed logs and dense shrubs, the hiking is awkward and tiring. Even now, close to the Bishop Glacier tributary, there is little hope for fording the deep, fast channel of the Pitt River.

We crash through scruffy forest to the edge of a rocky gully containing a turbulent glacial tributary stream. With no other way across, we are forced to pick our way carefully down the gully wall, facing inwards, using roots and branches for handholds. Feeling my calf muscles straining from my toe holds, I'm keenly aware that a slip could send me over a substantial drop into the Pitt River, or at very least, the glacial torrent. The gravelly soil soon softens, and I am able to kick my boots into firm footholds. Across the creek, we push through dense alder thickets and marshy ground for half an hour, coming out on the banks of the Pitt opposite the Bishop Glacier tributary.

I study the water, trying to gauge the depth. Several times I try wading out, but find the current too strong and the water well over a metre deep. We're going to have to head a ways upstream.

Having already endured so many hours of bushwhacking, the seemingly endless salmon-berry-covered rock slides are quickly becoming intolerable. The river doesn't change much for the first kilometre or so above my attempted crossing, but then it splits into several channels, spreading its water volume out into obviously shallower rapids. We find sturdy alder poles and change into running shoes. I undo the hip belt on my pack in case I have to dump it and swim — its weight would pull me under water. Once again, I seal my photo gear in its ziplock bag.

I start across. The first channel is easy and shallow. But the second requires some study to find a good crossing. The water is thigh deep, numbingly cold and strong, forcing me to lean heavily on the pole. Nearly knocked off balance by the current, I thrust forward to the rocks. This appears to have been the worst, so I start across the equally deep final channel. But my next step drops me into unexpectedly deep water. All my weight and strength go into holding my position against the current, my hands grasping the pole well under water. Even under the weight of my pack, my feet begin to float, and I can hear the hollow rumbling of rocks being pushed along the bottom by the current. At my limit, my right foot slips and I lunge for the overhanging alders and yank myself out of the water, numbed and tired from the cold and exertion. Having seen my difficulties, Greg looks undecided, then starts across warily. But even the second channel is too much for his shorter build. In a conversation shouted

Fording an unnamed tributary of the Pitt River

over the roar of the river, we decide to try to get a log across a narrow chute just downstream.

A half-hour of chopping with my ice axe gets me through a downed tree which I haul to the water's edge. I tie one end to the food cache rope and hurl the coiled rope across to Greg. He pulls the log across the main channel from the opposite bank in an attempt to make a footlog. But the centre touches the fast water and the log bounces madly up and down. It won't work. Again we shout over the roar, but nothing is decided. Finally Greg decides that he will go upstream to the forks first thing in the morning. We've split up the tent to distribute weight, so this means that we'll both sleep under the stars tonight. But the sky looks clear. We rig makeshift shelters and spend the night on opposite sides of the river.

Greg started upstream early this morning; I am in no hurry to get up. I pass the time sewing up my tattered pants, then decide to hike upstream to meet Greg. Somehow we miss each other, and when I return to my campsite, I find him already there. He had bushwhacked some two hours upstream to where the river forks, and avalanche snow bridges one channel.

We eat a little and then start the long, slow climb out of the Pitt River valley through forest, meadows and bluffy country to a high bench overlooking the Bishop Glacier moraine. Here, among idyllic sedge meadows and tiny streams, we find relaxation and relative silence after two long, hard days near the river. We pitch the tent by a clear pool, and cook a large pot of pasta. Tomorrow we will reach the trails again.

STRANGERS

The beautiful morning is marred only by the aggressive mosquitos, but the breeze sweeping down the valley from the glacier blows them away once we start walking. We drop through little meadow gullies to the long boulder slopes leading down to the creek. Now it is just a straightforward walk up the moraine to the snout of Bishop Glacier. Rounding the corner, the ice-draped bulk of Mount Garibaldi becomes visible at the head of the glacier, a familiar landmark that tells me our trek is nearly over. We begin the final grind up the steep valley side to the bluffs overlooking the meadows west of Mamquam Lake.

Drinking the clear water of a meltwater pool, I gaze out at the face of Mount Garibaldi across the clean white icefield. After a lengthy rest, in the long shadows of afternoon we wander down through the flowering meadows to Mamquam Lake and set up camp.

A land characterized by the sound of falling water

There are other hikers near the lake; columns of campfire smoke rise from the meadow patches near the shore. The people we pass say nothing, eyeing our swarthy faces and bush-worn clothing, perhaps wondering where we have been. It is quiet, with the gentle music of tumbling water sounding from across the lake. We set up camp and cook a large supper. I sort through my remaining food, burning the empty packages in a nearby fire pit. The lowering sun now paints the ramparts of Pyramid and Mamquam mountains in deepening shades of gold. The ripples fade from the lake, and its surface mirrors the glowing rock.

In the cool of morning we climb steadily up the trail towards the sunlight creeping down the meadows. From the ridge crest, the narrow thread of civilization stretches westwards across the barren moraines. Across flats below Lava Glacier where fifty years ago was ice. Across the flower-filled slopes of Opal Cone, and into the rocky valley where Ring Creek flows.

We meet a young park ranger, perhaps a university student on a summer job, who asks where we've been. I begin to describe our route, explaining that we started from Whistler, went over the back of the Spearhead Range, then followed the upper Cheakamus and Pitt rivers and a couple of high passes. But my description peters out; I can't imagine him really grasping my route description without a map. The places we've been, the creeks we've forded, the meadows and valleys we've walked and thrashed through, the waterfalls and glaciers we've seen, are mostly nameless corners of the wilderness. They are our wilderness experience. If he were to follow our route, his experience would be different than ours. Physically, it would be the same tract of country, but the emotional experiences that tie people to the land are always unique.

Still the young ranger's enthusiasm is encouraging. Greg and I wish him well and turn south towards Diamond Head, not for a second regretting the well-groomed trail, but knowing in our hearts that wilder places must remain.

EGIN

TIDEWATER TO TREELINE

Cruising north from Tofino towards the black clouds hanging over Obstruction Island, it seems only fitting that Clinton Webb is diligently waterproofing his boots. Up Millar Channel, the heavy drops begin to splatter across the windshield of the *Matlawhaw Pride*, and soon the calm water is blurred by the impact of a coastal downpour. Food packages bound for Ahousat and Hot Springs Cove, as well as our two backpacks, are frantically hauled into the cabin as the *Pride* races through the rock-lined reaches of Sulphur Passage.

When we have unloaded our gear, and stand on the rocks at the mouth of the Megin River watching the *Matlawhaw Pride* churn off down gloomy Shelter Inlet, the reality of our plan sets in. We will walk, without trails, up the Megin and across the mountains of Strathcona Provincial Park to Buttle Lake. It is a sixty-kilometre route that to our knowledge has never been walked in its entirety before. Standing in the rain, eyeing the impenetrable salmonberry thickets lining the river mouth, we content ourselves with the thought that matters can only improve.

Our plan had emerged from our mutual in-

terest in lowland old-growth forests, and the largest unlogged tract of rainforest remaining on Vancouver Island seemed a logical choice for a week-long trek. The added appeal of hiking through wilderness from ocean shore to alpine, halfway across the island, strengthened our desire to undertake the trip.

Clinton's background in ecology and forestry has given him an immense respect for, and understanding of, the complexity of natural cycles. But as a recreation and silvicultural technician with the B.C. Forest Service, he had become frustrated and disheartened by a system mired in outdated values and beliefs — a doctrine that placed immediate economic gain ahead of the ecological well-being of the land. Now working for meager pay with environmental groups, he applies his knowledge of this system to improving forestry practices and preserving wilderness.

Clinton and I examine the vague path leading into the bush. It goes some distance into the thicket, but then seems to end. We return through the soaked bush to the rocks and place our packs under a dense spruce tree. On our second, packless reconnaissance we pick up another path, closer to the river, which soon becomes more defined. We return for our packs, then strike off upriver, more confident about making some progress on this unusually miserable August evening.

As soon as the river water is shallow enough, we begin wading. Wearing our running shoes, we slosh upstream, following the wide gravel bars and crossing where the river washes from side to side. The water is warm and clear — lowland water born of rainfall and its slow release from the virgin rainforest. The rain streams down ceaselessly, but seeing Clinton shin-deep in the water — damp, bespectacled and clad in a yellow rainjacket and blue, fur-lined hat — carrying a plastic shopping bag full of home-grown vegetables, I find myself smiling at our situation.

"You look like a misplaced shopper who got lost on the weekly run to the supermarket!" He stops and smiles, explaining that with his wife away from home at the same time, the choice was between letting the leftovers go bad or bringing them along. "Well, it'll be nice having the extra vegetables for the first few days."

Two kilometres up from the mouth, the light fading, we pitch the tent under an overhanging bigleaf maple. After a simple cold dinner, we rest in our little dry haven while the rain drums on into the night.

UP THE RIVER

By morning the rain has stopped, and Clinton is already setting wet gear out on the rocks to dry. I do the same, then settle down for breakfast. All morning we make good progress up the river, generally wading, with the occasional romp through devil's club and salmonberry where a deep pool blocks our pas-

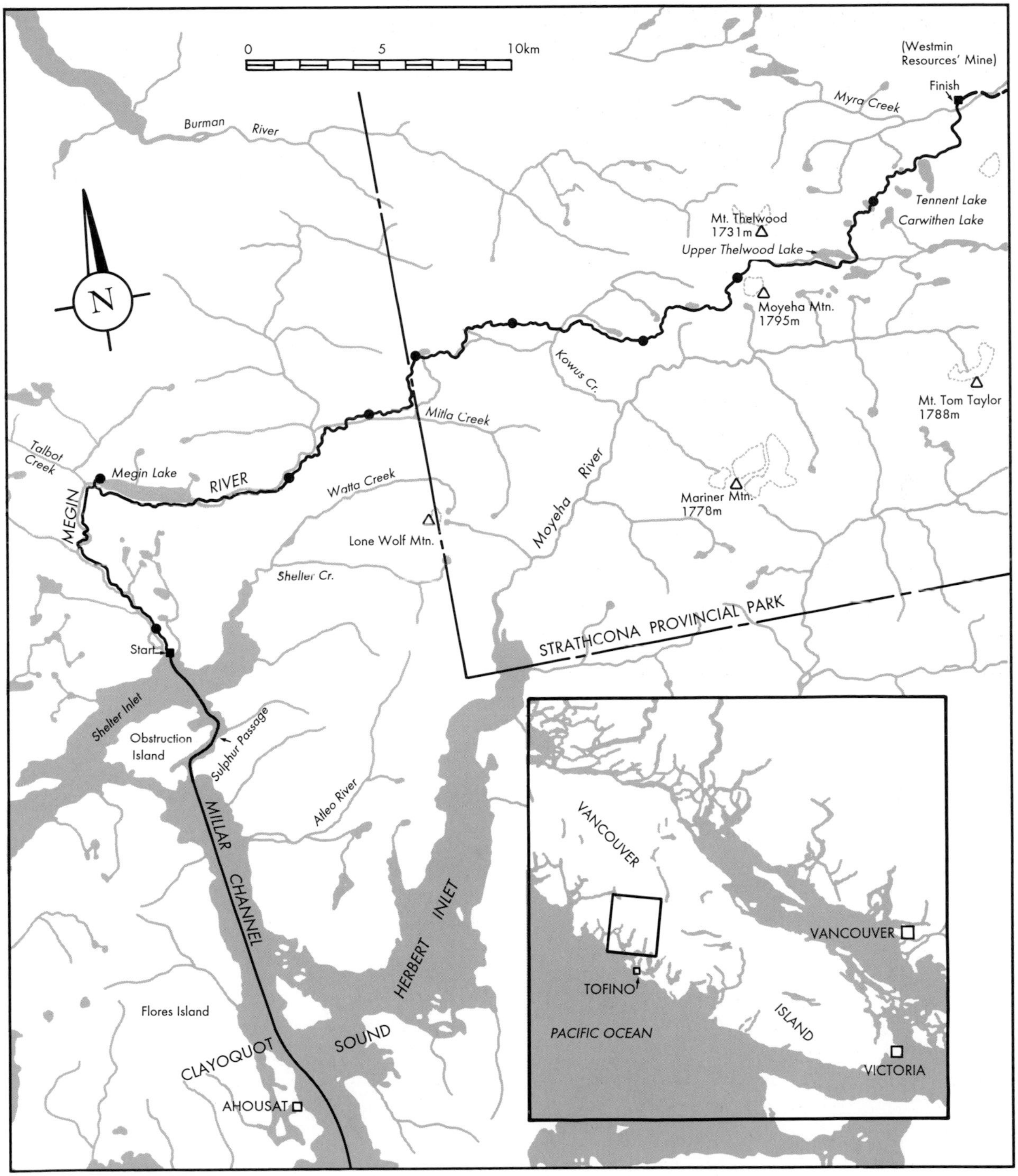

0   5   10km

N

Burman   River

Talbot Creek

MEGIN

Megin Lake   RIVER

Watta Creek

Mitla Creek

Lone Wolf Mtn.

Shelter Cr.

Kowus Cr.

Moyeha River

Mt. Thelwood 1731m

Upper Thelwood Lake

Moyeha Mtn. 1795m

Mariner Mtn. 1778m

Mt. Tom Taylor 1788m

Myra Creek

(Westmin Resources' Mine) Finish

Tennent Lake

Carwithen Lake

STRATHCONA   PROVINCIAL   PARK

Start

Shelter Inlet

Obstruction Island

Sulphur Passage

Atleo River

MILLAR   CHANNEL

Flores Island

CLAYOQUOT   SOUND

HERBERT   INLET

AHOUSAT

VANCOUVER

VANCOUVER

TOFINO

PACIFIC OCEAN

ISLAND

VICTORIA

Lower Megin River

sage in the river. Bald eagles wheel overhead; deer bounce along sandbars marked by wolf tracks and bear sign. Here we are guests in a wilderness that belongs to these creatures. And yet, I cannot help thinking, the 25,000 hectare Megin drainage, the largest complete, undeveloped watershed left on Vancouver Island, is threatened by logging interests that have taken one valley after another, cutting a swath that will lead inevitably to obliteration of our wilderness rainforests.

Shortly after lunch, a squall stops us beneath a convenient overhanging cedar tree. Out on the river, raindrops dimple the sunny water. As the rain dies, we shoulder our packs again and pick our way along the water's edge. I ford the river below the next big pool, then toss my stout driftwood pole back across to Clinton. This is one of the few places where the current is sufficient to warrant the use of a pole for balance.

The sun returns as we walk up long straight reaches of boulders between river bends. Unlike other west coast rivers, where lazy meanders are caused by water wandering from side to side across flat valley bottoms, the Megin's course seems more a result of the river's collisions with the abrupt valley sides. There are riverside groves of Douglas-fir here — a species more prevalent on the drier east side of Vancouver Island — along with the expected Sitka spruce, western redcedar and amabilis fir. Compared to other west coast valleys I've seen, the understorey is more varied too; bigleaf maple and vine maple arch above the river's edge, along with numerous ancient Pacific yew trees reaching for the light. Where we must walk through the forest, animal trails ease the passage through the undergrowth.

Our feet are growing weary from walking for hours on rocks in running shoes with heavy packs. But the curving valley ahead tells us that Megin Lake is not far off. Near the confluence of the Megin and Talbot Creek, we pause in the sun to study the aerial photos.

"The south side of Megin Lake looks better," says Clinton after a careful examination. "Lots of really steep, bluffy terrain on the north side." Nearby in the forest, behind two giant cedars, stands a small, hand-split shake cabin and shed. The door of the cabin — a single split-cedar slab — is off its hinges, and the inside is strewn with glass and old cans. Nevertheless, it appears not to have been disturbed for many years. "Prospectors," Clinton suggests, noting a piece of a drill core. "I wonder how they got a drill in here?" We disturb nothing and move on along a vague trail marked with brittle red survey tapes tied on galvanized nails. At the lake outlet, we wade across and bushwhack a short distance to the cabin we know stands nearby. A rustic sign on the door proclaims: "fishermen & travellers welcome here."

For the first time, we are plagued with mosquitos and no-see-ums. But the discomfort is forgotten as golden light falls on the forested mountains beyond Megin Lake. The clouds that have wrapped the mountains dissipate and reveal jagged fangs of rock thrusting up beyond the first ridge, above the headwaters of Watta Creek. On the gas stove we cook up some spaghetti complete with onions, garlic and green peppers from the vegetable bag. I sit back, throwing my feet up on the initial-carved top of the smokey cedar table.

"Maybe we should just stay here for a week," I say wistfully, gazing out at the forest-clad mountains mirrored in the waters of the lake. Clinton, stirring dinner between mosquito-squishing slaps, pauses for a moment. "Well, I'd want to bug-proof this cabin first!" A high pitched whirring and a needle prick in my neck

Old prospector's cabin

brings me back to reality. "Right!" I say on my way out the door to fetch water and photograph the glowing evening hills.

A LONG DAY IN THE SUN

It is a pleasant change to be walking in hiking boots after yesterday's long walk up the river in running shoes. We push into the forest on the south shore of Megin Lake. Clinton notes a cedar with an unusual square hole in its trunk. "Look at this! A CMT!" he says, using the abreviation for 'culturally modified tree.' "Wow! What a special place. Just imagine, perhaps a hundred years ago Native people were in here looking for canoe logs. Nice solid, healthy cedars." I step up and run my fingers over the axe marks which bear a delicate coating of moss, moist and soft like velvet. Around the test hole, which was cut to check the tree for soundness, lobes of new growth have partially closed the wound, placing a measure of time on the historic cut. "Could've been done a hundred years ago," I estimate. Around us stand a half-dozen other big cedars, forming a secluded little grove.

The sidehill soon steepens, and travel over windfalls and bushy, uneven ground is slow. For a while we follow a narrow beach along the lake, but are soon forced to return to the forest. Intermittent animal trails that tunnel under

A long day in the sun, upper Megin River

salal bushes and logs clearly show the lower profile of their makers as our packs snag on overhead branches. An old rock slide, its boulders sheathed in moss, gives us a break from the undergrowth for a while. Two-thirds of the way down the lake the beach resumes. Here the grasses are studded with wildflowers, and hundreds of sun-bleached drift logs have amassed between the forest and the shore. Among this natural debris, I find a few pieces of milled lumber and three old tires; perhaps a float at the cabin was blown apart during a storm, depositing these signs of human presence in this corner of the wilderness. We follow the curving shoreline past the drift logs and along the edge of a marsh to where river-deposited sand forms a hard beach. Here on the warm gravel of the river mouth, backed by pioneering alder trees, we stop for lunch. Clinton braves the water for a quick swim; I am content to lie on the clean gravel and absorb the sun's warmth.

After eating, we pull on our runners and begin to slosh up the river again. At each crossing the cool water refreshes my feet. Beyond the first bend, we mount a huge spruce log, then find ourselves jumping off the butt end into the river to reach a suitable crossing point. Seeing my performance — the heavy pack throws me off balance and I nearly fall back into the water on landing — Clinton passes down his pack before jumping. We scramble among roots along the river bank, then wade across to a wide gravel bar.

As we walk upstream, the lowering angle of the sun accentuates the beauty of this valley. Smooth gravel is backed by alder and maple trees, then by tall spruce and Douglas-fir which press up against the steep mountainsides. Unlike the high peaks, it does not feel cold and austere, but retains a certain mellowness and warmth. Continuing on up dry channels under the arching deciduous trees, we pass several perfect campsites where the river has deposited fine sand among the cobbles, but push on to make distance.

After a long bouldery stretch, we come to what the aerial photo shows is the last large gravel bar on the upper Megin — beyond the river narrows for good. A small patch of sand awaits our tent. As I rig a food cache in an old, overhanging yew tree, I notice another split-cedar cabin, nearly hidden from view atop a bluff beside the channel. A tiny outhouse is positioned so as to dump directly into the now-dry river channel below. "Clinton!" I call, knowing his fascination with old cabins. "Another cabin, complete with flush toilet!" "Oh, really?!" he says, scrambling up the bank, thinking aloud. "I've got to look at how this thing's built. There's something so special about finding stuff like this, way out in the bush, all built by hand. A real feeling of history."

There are no bugs tonight, and our little driftwood fire burns clean and hot into the night. As it begins to die, a few raindrops fall.

MITLA CREEK

Early in the morning, I can hear the steady patter of rain on the tent fly. I drift off again, feeling no urge to force myself out of the sleeping bag. An hour or so later, I awake again to the gentle rushing of the Megin. The damp sand outside is drying under a tentative sun. We pack up and cook breakfast in the shelter of the overhanging yew tree below the cabin.

The off-and-on drizzle passes almost unnoticed. As we begin to walk towards the end of the bar, it brightens again, and we are soon penetrating the rain-drenched bush. Thick devil's club and towering huckleberry bushes grow under the lofty canopy of a moss-padded hemlock-amabilis fir forest. Here and there stand large, well-shaped cedars. One is three metres thick and rises with gently tapering perfection into the canopy.

For two hours we push through this forest. At times the sun breaks through, and the bushes seem laden with thousands of sparkling diamonds. We emerge from the woods onto slick, water-polished granite where the Megin issues from a canyon. Centuries of slow erosion have worn the hard rock into smooth saucers and ridges. The river itself slows into a pool lined by rock formations. The green water, perhaps ten metres deep, eddies slowly among overhanging sculptures of rock.

The forest above the canyon is mostly cedar and hemlock with moderate underbrush. After climbing onto a benchland where large cedars predominate, we travel through thick, rain-soaked bush, slithering and scrambling over and under windfalls, towards Mitla Creek which joins the Megin from the east. The bushwhack drags on, with the increasing roar of the creek hinting at a canyon we had not anticipated. Indeed, Mitla Creek rushes urgently down a steep gash in the rainforest. We turn upstream, working our way down towards the water wherever possible. When we finally reach the creek, we are overdue for a good drink and lunch.

The Mitla is a fast-flowing stream which drops rapidly among huge boulders. Hemmed in by steep ridges, it is a gloomy place in this unsettled weather, a damp and foreboding pit of a rainforest valley that today is like the back side of hell. But such places have character; they live and breathe and ooze with the mist of sun on rain-soaked needles. These places were not made for humans, they were made for the myriad other life forms that inhabit the deep forest. Thousands of years, unburned, uncut,

Cedar-hemlock rainforest near Mitla Creek

rotting and renewing until the air within is so rich with the aroma of humus and heavy with its mist that it is like biological soup. Mosses, ferns and lichens sprout from every surface on which moisture condenses. Logs — sound, or fragile shells of humus — lie jackstrawed atop one another. Branches, twigs, needles, cones, leaves, stems: a metre of accumulated forest litter. This is the temperate rainforest — not just big trees, but little trees growing on big trees growing on fallen trees lying atop rotted trees, all linked in an unbroken chain of life thousands of years long.

We clamber over and under massive deadfalls, often having to climb straight up the forty-five-degree mountainside, hanging on to ferns and shrubs. Then we pick up an animal trail which guides us through the canyon. As

Licorice ferns on a maple branch

the terrain eases, the trail fades out, leaving us in a thicket of devil's club. Clinton peers through the latticework of heavily-armed stems, wiping foggy glasses as if he doesn't believe his eyes. "What kind of animal would make a trail that dead-ends in devil's club?" he asks. On the valley floor the gradient is now shallow, but the ground is uneven, frequently littered with moss- and bush-covered boulders, remnants of long-ago rock slides.

Carefully wading over sharp, submerged stones, we cross to the north side of turbulent Mitla Creek. Here we forge on for a half-hour through very dense huckleberry and old rock slides, then begin to look for a campsite. There are no flat spots large enough for our tent in the forest, but a small island in the creek offers a dry channel with a sand patch. "Well, Mitla Creek now has a total of one flat campsite!" I joke, while methodically levelling a tent platform with my boot. Here, in this bug-infested rainforest, we cook under the extra tarp, itching, swatting and cursing pointlessly at the persistent no-see-ums. Our carefully preserved bug-free environment — the tent — seems incredibly peaceful as I lie in my bag listening to the creek. After three full days, we are deep in the wilderness, cloistered away in this narrow valley full of tumultuous growth, and despite the bugs and rain and bush, I can only hope that it will always remain wild as I have seen it.

TO THE HIGH COUNTRY

Clinton and I have walked for only five minutes up the dry channel when we face this morning's bushwhack. There is a peculiar sense of pleasure as we plunge with little hesitation into the drenched salmonberry and work our way to the dense forest beyond. After four days of rugged wilderness travel, our bodies and minds are fully tuned to this, to the point where normal discomforts, like damp clothes or a slap in the face by a soaking wet branch, go almost unnoticed. Exploratory bushwhacking has almost become a lost art with the steady demise of forested wilderness. Accounts of early explorations are riddled with the horrors of coastal bush, and today's explorers, given technological alternatives, too often seem content to avoid this aspect of wilderness altogether. We lose something of the spirit that way, I feel, for the added elements of coping with the physical and mental challenges found in the lowlands enrich the experience, even if they do also infuriate one at times.

The bush remains thick even under the heavy canopy of the coniferous trees. As we meander around looking for openings, I pick up a long series of bush-free patches in the ancient hemlock forest. Occasionally, giant rotting Douglas-fir snags loom up through the misty

Bracket fungus

greenery, signposts pointing to a long-forgotten history of forest fires.

All morning we hike through the wet bush — poison-spined devil's club and thick, head-high huckleberry that showers us as we push it aside — soaked boots squelching and bodies sweating within rain gear. Clinton gazes upwards at the dripping vegetation, smiling and commenting enthusiastically. "Isn't it interesting how this is so enjoyable? It's as if something happens physiologically or psychologically after several days into a bushwack like this." "Yeah," I grin, "we start to go nuts!"

Rising gradually across the sidehill, we aim towards the creek that drains today's destination, a subalpine lake at one-thousand metres atop the ridge north of Mitla Creek. The creek cascades down over slabs of bedrock in a small canyon bordered by a ridge of open forest. The ridge is steep, but the lack of bush makes walking easy. Above is a cliff band which runs the entire length of the valley. Using trees and roots for support, we clamber up a bushy cleft in the bluffs, straining and forcing our bloated packs through the tightly spaced little trees. The sun now filters through the foliage. Minutes later, Clinton breaks out onto an open bluff above a waterfall. There is no question about whether to stop here for lunch. We eat while gazing out over the green cleft of Mitla Creek two hundred metres below; shreds of mist still hang in the rainforest, but up here we sit in the warm sun.

Clinton checks his altimeter and looks at me with a puzzled expression. "We're at four-hundred and fifty metres. According to the map," he pauses to double check, "the creek makes a sharp bend at just over three-hundred metres." I study the map while eating. "We must have climbed up this creek here, one too soon. Shouldn't really matter, as long as it doesn't get too steep. The contours look a little tight."

Despite our error, this turns out to be a good route through open forest, with huge wet huckleberries to quench our thirst. Soon we are on open bluffs, dotted with yellow-cedar and lodgepole pine. As the bluffs steepen, I make a re-

The lunch spot above Mitla Creek

connaissance without my pack, finding a feasible route to the ridge top. "Looks a bit tricky," Clinton notes, not having the mountaineering background that I do. From above I can see that there is only one difficult spot — a little rock step where my greater reach enabled me to grasp a good hold. "Why don't you tie your pack to the food cache rope?" I suggest. "I'll pull it up and you can climb that little step without your pack. The rest is easy." We work our way up to the top, where heather meadows appear among the rocks.

For much of the climb out of Mitla Creek we have been criss-crossing the western boundary of Strathcona Park. As we begin to traverse towards the lake on the ridge above Mitla Creek, we leave behind the endangered Megin River wilderness and enter the less-threatened park-land. Throughout its history, Strathcona — established in 1911 as British Columbia's first provincial park — has been abused; dams have flooded its lakes, forests have been traded away to logging interests, and mineral claims allowed to poison the sanctity of this parkland. Here we are in a nature conservancy zone, but our destination — Westmin Resources' mine — reminds us that park protection is only as good as the vigilance of conservationists and the will of politicians.

August 15 begins clear and cool, a strikingly beautiful morning quickly being warmed by the sun. Remnant clouds stream from the jagged peaks to the north. South, across the socked-in headwaters of Mitla Creek, sharp fangs of rock tear through the remains of heavy winter snow-pack. Our unnamed lake shines lead-silver in its little basin. Clinton has strung a long clothes-line, and our damp gear is hanging or lies spread across the rocks to dry. We break out cameras and tripods and photograph the wilderness emerging from the rainstorm.

"It is so good to be in shorts and have a dry pack!" Clinton exclaims as we begin hiking east along the lake shore. "What a luxury after two days in soaked rain gear!" I smile at how such a simple thing can bring great pleasure. Our route takes us up a ridge to the southeast of the lake, past a smaller lake, and around the mountain shoulder to a narrow divide which separates Mitla Creek — part of the Megin drainage — from a western fork of Kowus Creek, a tributary of the Moyeha River. We de-

Unnamed lake at one thousand metres north of Mitla Creek

scend the large avalanche chute on the Kowus side, cross residual snow near the bottom and climb through slide-battered trees onto a small, heather-covered knoll. Clinton heads for the rim of the bluff for a lunchtime view of the valley, but as he crests a hump, he pivots around and runs back towards me shouting.

"Shit! There's a bear! Right there, behind that knoll! A black bear and a cub!"

"I thought you stepped on a hornet's nest or something," I reply, only then feeling a flush of adrenalin as I hear the cussing and grunting of the mother bear's warning and see a little black cub swaying cutely above the hump in a treetop. Concious of the increased thumping in my chest, I resist the temptation to move in and photograph the cub. We turn around and quickly traverse the mountainside to a rocky creek gully. Sufficiently distant from bruin, we break out lunch.

We intend to continue traversing around the head of the valley to a narrow bench which merges with a bluffy ridge leading all the way down to the main stem of Kowus Creek. Starting out again, we clamber up a steep gravel bank out of the creek gully, then drop right back down into another gully beyond. For half an hour we traverse steep slide gullies, their sides thick with slide alder and blueberry bushes. Crossing one slick slope, my foothold gives away and I rapidly accelerate down the gully. Almost immediately, my arm lashes out instinctively and snatches an alder branch, bringing me to an abrupt halt.

On the treed ridges between gullies are large mountain hemlock and yellow-cedar trees, often twisted and battered by winter avalanches. Beyond a tedious moss-covered rock slide, we encounter two enormous yellow-cedars. The larger tree, three metres in diameter, is a near-record-size for the species. Even if it isn't the largest, it surely is one of the most remote giants left, for here we are in the heart of the greatest tract of wilderness left on Vancouver Island, at least four days' travel from the nearest road.

The near-record-sized yellow-cedar (*Clinton Webb*)

For two hours we thrash through extremely dense subalpine forest — the most difficult bushwhacking so far on the trip — up gullies, over bluffs, through fragrant thickets of prickly, abrasive yellow-cedar krummholz, then back down again with the realization that we have traversed too high into a cliff belt. With great relief, we finally pick up the treed bench and emerge in the ridge-top meadows, the light fading. We reach a tiny lake and set up camp as tentative raindrops begin to fall from the darkening sky.

UP AND DOWN DAY

The threatened rain did not materialize overnight, and I awake to a sun-warmed tent. With the now-standard bug protection on — ski hats, mitts and, for me, a head net — Clinton and I examine the air photos during our leisurely breakfast and packing routine. The route ahead looks good, but it will be an up-and-down day, as we must cross the deep valley of Kowus Creek, a descent of 550 metres followed by a 450-metre climb up the other side.

Strolling through meadows among bluffs, we soon begin to descend towards Kowus Creek, rarely without views of the forested valley curving

Moyeha River valley

off southeast towards the distant Moyeha. Our hiking is frequently interrupted by stops to feast off heavily laden huckleberry bushes.

The terrain here is very rugged and rich in contrasts between extensive rocky ridges and lush mountainside forests. There is much exposed bedrock, and shallow soils support stunted lodgepole pine and Douglas-fir. Pockets in the bluffs cradle little pools dotted with water lilies. The ridge descends abruptly into a rich lowland forest of large western redcedar and thick moss.

Negotiating one last tricky cliff band, we ramble down to the open, bouldery creek bed. "What a special place!" remarks Clinton. "Such an utterly untouched creek draining all this wilderness, then flowing down into the Moyeha, pristine all the way to the ocean. This is exactly the kind of place I'd like to build an unobtrusive little cabin, just inside the forest, beside the creek."

After lunch beside the clear waters of Kowus Creek, we cross and hike through damp cedar forest to a shallow ridge between two creeks. Climbing through easy forest, the ridge opens up to heather patches and little rock bluffs. Bypassing a lake at one-thousand metres, we emerge on a ridge overlooking the Moyeha River valley. Clinton feels a lack of energy this afternoon, so we discuss how far to continue. Recognizing both the need to make distance and Clinton's condition, we push on only as far

as the open bluffs on the rim of the Moyeha. Here we set up camp beside a dark pool. All day the cloud cover has thickened, and now a heavy sheet of overcast blankets the peaks.

MOYEHA

On this glorious morning, we gaze out from our bluff over the Moyeha Valley. From the estuary at distant Herbert Inlet to the gleaming glaciers of Mariner Mountain, all is bathed in clear morning sunlight. From this great gulf rises the river's roar, the voice of the wilderness. The Moyeha is special, for it is the only major west coast river drainage south of Alaska that is both totally undeveloped from ocean shore to treeline and entirely within a park. The only one.

"Incredible!" I say, instantly realizing the inadequacy of the word. I join Clinton for breakfast on the rocks. He's already going on about building a cabin down by the Moyeha. "Geez, if you had your way, there'd be no wilderness left, with all your cabins littered everywhere!"

We climb for an hour through easy forest and over bluffs to a meadowed gap in the ridge

Hiking towards Moyeha Mountain

crest. To the north, a pretty hourglass-shaped lake nestles in a narrow valley, its deep blue waters nearly divided by a rock isthmus. Looking at the warm rocks, I promise myself a swim today. Beyond the gap the bluffs steepen. As I reach the top, I hear Clinton's shouts.

"Randy! I'm stuck! Help! I don't know how long I can hold on!" I feel a prick of fear, then a surge of adrenalin. "Hang on! I'm coming!" He has climbed up a little gully into an awkward position where he can move neither up nor down safely. With the weight of his pack pulling him, his arms are quickly fatiguing and he is in danger of falling. I quickly drop my pack and clamber down to a position just above him. Bracing my feet, I give him my outstretched arm. "Here. Hang on!"

This incident serves as a reminder of how easy it would be to turn the joy of exploration into an exercise in survival. A serious injury here, a good four days' travel from help, could put us in a life-threatening situation. This is a risk that we accept as part of wilderness travel, but not without a great deal of respect for the unpredictable environment in which we live.

Minutes later we are on the high ridges north of the Moyeha Valley. In the distance to the north, I can see the highest ramparts of Vancouver Island — the Golden Hinde, Elkhorn and Colonel Foster. Directly to the east is the pyramid of Moyeha Mountain. Scrambling through a series of little valleys between bluffs, we find our swimming hole — a long clear lake tucked against a vertical wall of rock. We do not hesitate, quickly stripping and plunging naked into the frigid water. "Woooh, woooh, woooh! Woooh, woooh, woooh!" Our shouts reverberate off the rock walls.

Afterwards, sitting in the sun, we are accosted by whining mosquitos and inspired by the pure echo. In the spontaneous, uninhibited way of good friends, we begin a series of mock announcements. "Attention all hikers! hikers, hikers . . . by order of the Minister of Parks! parks, parks . . . A chemical-spraying mosquito control program! program, program . . . has

Sunset over Moyeha Mountain

been itiiated for Strathcona Provincial Park!! park, park, park." Joking and laughing in the echo chamber, it hasn't totally escaped us that such a program wouldn't be at all surprising in B.C.'s oldest, most abused provincial park. But today, it's all in jest.

East of the lake, our route takes us through a scenic gap and across a snowfield to the rim of a great cirque below Moyeha Mountain. We had intended to drop down to cross, but it is now evident that the descent would be very steep, and the subsequent elevation gain on the opposite side equally so. After some debate, we decide to try the ridge crest above. Rounded rock domes punctuate this ridgeline, the highest point on our route, a 1,430-metre-high skywalk between the great cirque to the northwest and the roaring vastness of the Moyeha. In the lowering sun of afternoon, the western mountains take on an impressionistic quality, like a Toni Onley painting. For most of this day, we have walked along the northern divide of the only completely protected major river system on Vancouver Island. I have felt its presence, wild and mysterious, and taken comfort from the knowledge that this valley, at least, we will leave for the future.

Subalpine gardens

We ramble along the crest to a gap that leads us down to the north. I boot ski down a snowfinger, then traverse a series of wide, bushy ledges. Clinton follows, and together we emerge on the barren, boulder-strewn plateau northwest of Moyeha Mountain. We select a campsite near one of dozens of deep pools, then cook dinner as the setting sun's amber light climbs the peaks and slips off into the night.

OVER THE DIVIDE

Clinton is standing pondering his two shirts lying on the rocks. Scratching his bearded chin, he mutters something about "amazing."

"Hey, Randy, look at this! Remember how yesterday I had a swarm of mosquitos around me after I changed into my blue shirt?" He gestures towards the rock. The navy blue shirt is covered with a seething swarm of mosquitos, while the beige one is almost free of them. "Maybe it's the lighter colour," I guess, recalling how fiercely the bugs were attacking me in my own navy blue shirt — my only colour choice. "Something to remember, isn't it?"

Another sunny morning sees us hiking around the ridge to the north, gently descending heather slopes into the meadowed valley that leads east towards the head of Thelwood Creek. A short climb among boulders and wildflowers brings us to the Vancouver Island divide. Here we leave the westward flowing drainage of Kowus Creek and begin to descend into the valley of Thelwood Creek, which drains east into the Strait of Georgia. Below the pass, a flat gravel wash supports a brilliant display of wildflowers. Patches of lupines, Indian paintbrush, daisies, and monkeyflowers splash their brilliance across the valley floor, while the creek flows clear and shallow into a little gorge. After negotiating this gap, we again ramble across gravel washes and heather slopes, following Thelwood Creek to its delta at beautiful Upper Thelwood Lake. Here, for the first time since our last camp along the Megin five days ago, we can relax without mosquitos. It is such a luxury to lie in the sun unmolested by the little bloodsuckers!

Upper Thelwood Lake

The last evening above Carwithen Lake

Along the south shore of Upper Thelwood Lake, I also see the first signs of human presence since the Megin; a tiny scrap of red plastic mesh lies beside my boot. Then, over a rise, there is a ladderlike series of planks nailed to a yellow-cedar, perhaps a survey marker of some kind. Near the east end of the lake, a faint trail appears, and I note the imprint of a Vibram sole.

After lunch beside the lake, we climb again into the steep, bluffy high country between Thelwood and Myra creeks. Our route takes us over a rocky spur and past the outlet of an unnamed lake. Then we ascend to a gentle ridge overlooking Carwithen Lake and drop down a snow gully to a second, more picturesque, unnamed lake. A dead-level sedge patch beside the outlet creek makes a perfect final campsite for the trip.

Sitting by the lake outlet, where a fitful breeze keeps the bugs away, I note an amber reflection across the water. Glancing behind me, I am startled by the burning orange glaciers of Mount Tom Taylor, every crevasse and subtle undulation etched in fine detail by the long shadows of the setting sun. Here, on our last night out, the wilderness gives us its finest display of alpenglow. I hurry down to the tent for my camera, then dash up to a bluff for a better view. But just as my telephoto lens clicks into place, the colour fades suddenly as the sun drops behind the mountains. Perhaps it is right for this moment to be etched into my memory by a missed photo. This way I will remember, not merely recall at the sight of a photo, this special night in Strathcona Park.

COMING HOME

August 19 will be our final day in the wilderness that has become our short-term home. But here the images of beauty are punctuated by sadness. From the high plateau we can see the dam and road at Jim Mitchell Lake, only a few kilometres to the east, and the exhaust-fan drone and massive scar of the Westmin Resources mine spoils the country around Myra Creek. We wander through a maze of little bluffs and meadows, past a string of tiny lakes. Then we crest the final divide, hike around a meadow-ringed pond, and drop through forest along a stream towards Tennent Lake. Breaking out of the trees, it is clear that Tennent is not really a lake as mountain lakes should be. A dam blocks the outlet, and fluctuating water levels have stained the shoreline with rings like those on a toilet bowl. The level is down, exposing silty grey stumps and debris. We walk quietly past the dam and down the rocky pipeline track. On and on, down the steep mountainside, following the green-painted pipe, the drone of the mine steadily becoming louder, we descend. Near the bottom, majestic Douglas-firs line the track, but they do not have the same power when the constant whine of generators replaces the gentle music of wind in the treetops.

Despite these intrusions, much of Strathcona is still the wild and beautiful heartland of Vancouver Island. For eight out of our nine days, Clinton and I hiked through country virtually unchanged by modern civilization. With adjacent areas such as the Megin protected, there would still be hope that what we experienced could be enjoyed by generations yet unborn, so that they might also know the island as it was, from tidewater to treeline.

POSTSCRIPT

In April 1993, the entire Megin River drainage, as well as adjacent Watta and Shelter creeks, were added to Strathcona Provincial Park, part of a controversial provincial government land use decision on Clayoquot Sound. The wilderness between the Megin, adjacent Sydney Inlet and Flores Island, which comprises one of the largest undisturbed tracts of temperate rainforest left in North America, remains open to logging.

$\mathcal{S}$*TEIN*

HIGH RIDGE RAMBLINGS

*T*he dusty logging road rambles past jade green lakes and decimated forests. Green sweeps of marshland seem out of place amid the fresh brown logging slash. High on a mountain shoulder, a yellow steel spar sits poised to yard in yet another clearcut's timber.

Joe Foy lazily pilots his truck, bouncing and rattling along through this all-too-familiar portrait of B.C. "wilderness." This is the valley of Kwoiek Creek, one of the western tributaries of the Fraser River, which drains the leeward slopes of the Coast Mountains into the Fraser Canyon between Boston Bar and Lytton. One

valley north of Kwoiek is the Stein. Unlike its neighbouring valleys, the Stein is still wilderness. Only a primitive trail penetrates its heart, and its tributaries — Cottonwood, Scudamore and Rutledge creeks, and dozens of smaller streams — flow from the snowfields and glaciers through remarkably diverse wild forests that are home to grizzly bear, black bear, wolverine, mountain lion, moose, deer and other inhabitants of the wilderness.

Because of its location in the transition zone between coastal and interior climate patterns, the 109,000-hectare Stein drainage spans

Ponderosa pine bark

six of the fourteen biogeoclimatic zones in British Columbia, from the alpine tundra and wet coastal western hemlock in the west to the semi-arid ponderosa pine-bunchgrass near the mouth at the Fraser River.

In the mid-1980s, in the midst of a polarized debate over whether to log or preserve the Stein, an old prospector's trail up the lower Stein River was re-cleared and extended to Stein Lake near the head of the valley, and a primitive alpine route was marked over the divide to a logging road at Lizzie Lake, east of Pemberton. Hikers began to traverse the valley on a regular basis, but the overwhelming sense of wildness was not significantly diminished.

That wildness has captivated thousands of people over a still-unfinished, eighteen-year struggle to save the Stein from logging. Many will never walk the rugged backcountry, but nevertheless take comfort from knowing that its wilderness still exists.

On this calm August day, Leo DeGroot, my brother Greg and I unload our gear at the end of the Kwoiek Creek logging road and make final preparations for a different traverse of the Stein — nearly one-hundred kilometres north and east along high ridges and down the lower Stein Valley to Lytton.

Tall, lean and witty, Leo has spent many weeks in the Stein, hiking, ski-touring, building trails and working with the Rediscovery program teaching children wilderness skills. This trip is a return to a wilderness he knows well. Nonetheless, much of our route will be through new territory where none of us have ventured before.

Joe's truck rumbles off down the fractured landscape of Kwoiek, and the three of us are left alone on the desolate landing amid slash-burned logging debris. For the first few minutes we make our way up fire-blackened logging slash, tiptoeing around and over charred logs, getting used to the weight of our heavy packs and working out the stiffness and kinks from the four-hour drive from Vancouver. Settling into a rhythm, the going improves as we enter an open forest of Engelmann spruce, sub-alpine fir and lodgepole pine, occasionally broken by rock bluffs covered by chipmunk-cracked cone scales and thick needle duff. We soon pick up a vague trail, passing the remains of an old lean-to that suggests this route was established by trappers many years ago. Avalanche chutes — mossy, fern-filled glades — break the forest which soon gives way to a wide slide path. We work our way among slide alder thickets, boulders and battered mountain hemlock trees to the margin of a beaver swamp that covers the valley floor. On the grass-covered mound of an ancient beaver lodge stands a fully grown tree, perhaps 120 years old, testimony to the long tenure of these inhabitants of this little corner of the world.

For an hour beyond the swamp we penetrate dense rhododendron thickets on a steep

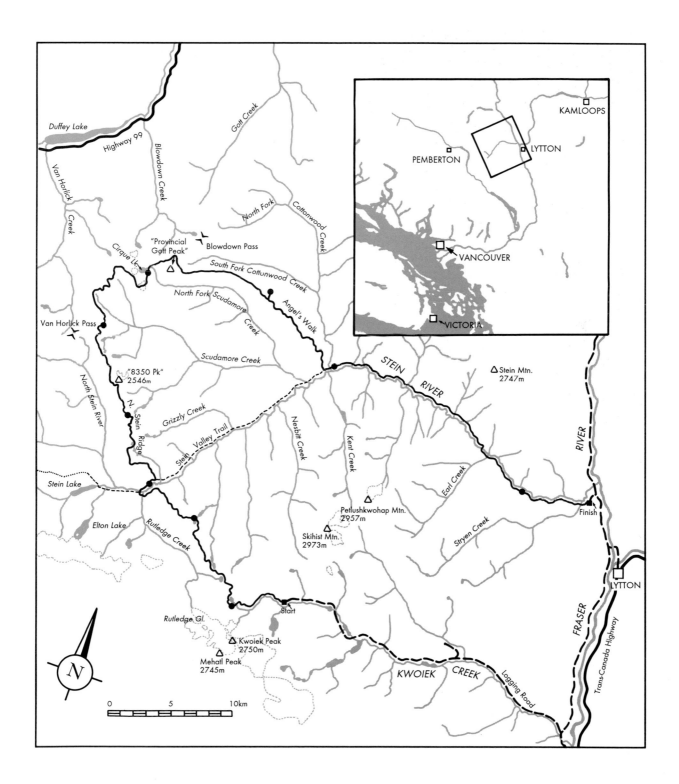

Forest hiking, upper Kwoiek Creek

mountainside — making for slow travel and sore feet from walking on the sidehill. Rain squalls pass, followed by periods of sunshine. Stopping for a snack, Leo pulls out the topographical map.

"Why don't we start climbing up to treeline? If we angle up now, we'll come out near this lake at 1,950 metres where we could camp. Probably avoid a lot of bushwhacking." Greg and I agree.

Starting up, openings in the forest — heather meadows and rock bluffs — are a welcome change from the bush, offering views of the glacier-hung north wall of Kwoiek Peak at the head of the valley. Damp draws and bluffs dotted with whitebark pines lead upwards to a high cirque containing the unnamed alpine lake. We set up camp near the lake outlet. Leo and I pitch a lightweight tent, while Greg rigs his three-by-four-metre nylon tarp. The dinnertime view from camp is of Kwoiek Peak and its glaciers under the lowering sun. To the northwest, above the lake and still hidden from our view, lies the Stein Valley. The sky is now mostly clear, promising a good day for tomorrow's trek over the divide.

ACROSS THE LINE

The three of us climb across the talus slopes above the unnamed lake which sparkles in the clear morning sunlight. Above the talus, we clamber up among bluffs, meadow patches, barren scree and krummholz — dense thickets of evergreen trees severely stunted by wind and blowing snow. From the pass, we have our first view northward across the imaginary line into the Stein River drainage. Directly below to the north, the indigo disk of another unnamed lake forms the foreground to a scene of meadowed ridges, steep forested valleys and subalpine lakes. Not a single sign of human presence is visible.

We angle to the northeast, walking down across a huge rock slab to a small snowfield among the boulders. A short glissade — boot skiing — followed by a long scramble among rocks and flowering meadow patches, brings us to the shore of the lake. Leo braves the frigid waters for a swim, as Greg and I recline on the big, warm rocks at the water's edge, eating "gorp" — trail mix of nuts and dried fruit — and drinking the pure water. The simple joy of being in the wild with like-minded companions has begun to sink in. With none of the diversions of everyday life — chores or projects that "have to be done" — both exercise and total relaxation come naturally. On average in the mountains, we spend seven to nine hours a day being physically active, occasionally interrupted by an hour or two of peaceful contemplation in a particularly pleasant spot. Often we are climbing up steep slopes, working the body, raising the heart rate, while carrying twenty-five kilogram loads, all in clean mountain air. I find the mellow tiredness felt at the end of such days is among the purest forms of relaxation.

After a half-hour of easy walking through pleasant meadows and resin-scented subalpine forest groves, we round the west side of the first of two long, shallow lakes. No sooner have we stopped between the lakes, and Leo is again stripping down for another swim.

We fill our water bottles for the dry ridge

Boulder walking above Rutledge Creek

ahead, then climb to the crest. Wind-battered spruce and pine trees line up along the windward edge of the ridgeline, where winter snow is shallow and melts rapidly in spring, extending the growing season just long enough for tree growth. To the west, the great forested gulf of Rutledge Creek valley drops away into massive space. Rambling for an hour along the high skyline to the north, we reach a ridge overlooking a rocky, pine-studded basin cradling a chain of pretty lakes. "Well, there's our campsite for tonight!" I announce, eyeing a little peninsula in the upper lake.

We start the long descent, running and sliding down a loose scree slope — the hollow, tinkling noise this makes sounds like an entire shipment of dinner plates being smashed. The remainder of the walk down over loose, angu-

lar, granite boulders is more tedious, and it is a relief to reach the undulating heather meadows on the valley floor. At the highest lake, we drop our packs and settle down on the big rock slabs sloping into the water. Atop the outcrops, twisted whitebark pines and subalpine firs find crevices into which to sink their roots.

Our campsite is a perfect spot among heather patches and pine needle-padded rock slabs. Across a draw on a bluff, an ancient pine with a thick horizontal limb — like a hangman's tree of the old west — makes a perfect place to hang our food cache.

Big, twisted whitebark pines in a basin below catch my attention. I scramble down to inspect the trees, finding the biggest to be one and a half metres in diameter — a new record for this species in B.C. Its scaly-barked trunk is adorned with burls, and the whole base sprouts on an angle from the slope, perhaps the legacy of heavy snow bending it over when it was a sapling. Whitebark pines isolated from fire on dry, subalpine slopes may live for over seven hundred years. This monarch has certainly witnessed the passing of a few centuries.

Evening falls over the boulder basin, which echoes with the melodic sound of falling water. Light cloud cover has developed, but the mood is still warm and friendly. I lie in my sleeping bag thinking about my girlfriend halfway around the world on another wild mountain. After a while, I drift off, anticipating the morning's long descent to the Stein River.

THE RIVER

Two hundred and fifty metres above camp we stand on the ridge overlooking the upper canyon of the Stein River. The river itself, still hidden in the narrow valley bottom, makes only a distant rushing sound. "A thousand metres down to the river," says Leo. "Let's head down to that neat little meadow with the pond. According to the map, there should be a gully leading down from there." Eroded gravel material from a stream gully has spread across the picturesque sedge meadow and stands out in contrast to the surrounding green. To the east, unusual light-coloured scree slopes seem strangely out of place among the darker bluffs — a striking, desert-like landform in the coastal mountains.

Heather-carpeted gullies lead down in a great staircase towards a tributary creek which drains into the Stein. Soon stands of subalpine fir and Engelmann spruce begin to close in, and we crash through thickets of willow beneath the evergreens. We make fast progress down the mountainside, which steepens into a series of bluffs and rock slides. The forest becomes drier as we emerge from the tributary valley, with Douglas-fir appearing among the spruce and subalpine fir. Windfallen trees and seepage areas thick with poison-spined devil's club slow our progress, but the pull of the river, now roaring from below, keeps us eagerly moving downward.

From a bluff we finally glimpse the milky green waters of the Stein River coursing through stands of tall, spire-shaped Engelmann spruce on the flat valley bottom. Another twenty minutes through forest thick with windfall brings us to the valley floor where we push through dense, swampy willow thickets towards the light of the river opening. A few minutes later, crowded into a little open space on the clay bank, we observe the river at close range for the first time, noting its depth and swiftness. No logs span the channel.

"I doubt we can ford that," notes Greg realistically. Leo pulls out his map. "We can hike upstream, see if there're any logs across, and if not, go to the cable car. It's about a kilometre, but we'll have to cross Rutledge Creek," he says, referring to the hand-operated aluminum cable car where the Stein Valley trail crosses the river just above Rutledge Creek. Leo leads on, moving efficiently through the tangled brush. Rutledge Creek is also running high, but its glacial waters are spread out into the willow and alder thickets by a log jam. Leo and I reconnoitre the crossing without our packs, carefully walking a series of slender logs — some bobbing in the current. Returning with the packs, we gingerly work our way across, struggling through a maze of toppled trees along the creek bank. A short walk through the forest brings us to the cable car across the Stein. One by one, we cross the river, gratefully accepting this little piece of technology, but also aware that it has eliminated a challenge we would have faced in a totally primitive land.

For the first time in days, I can walk with even strides on a trail — a thin ribbon of civilization. The path edges the base of the mountainside and enters a pretty little cedar grove, damp, musty and fragrant. Not far beyond, a side trail leads across a log over a slough to Island Camp, a small sandbar on a bend of the Stein. In the cool of evening we cook beside the gently swirling and bubbling river as the line of shadow creeps up the steep mountainside to the north. Tomorrow, we too will creep ever so slowly up that mountainside to the North Stein Ridge.

NORTH STEIN

The valley floor still lies in cool morning shadow as we break camp and walk the dew-dampened forest trail to the base of the mountain. Our slow, steady climb begins through open stands of lodgepole pine and Douglas-fir. Here, the sandy ground is littered with needles, cones, crackling dry sticks and small windfalls. Clusters of small, cone-shaped depressions in the sandy soil arouse my curiosity. These are the traps of ant lions, insect larvae which feed on ants and other insects which slide into the cones, unable to escape up the loose, sandy sides. After they pupate in the soil, the adults transform into winged insects similar to damselflies.

Small bluffs offer views back towards Rutledge Creek, flowing from the south, across the Stein. The forest thickens, and windfalls become frequent. Every now and then, large fire-scarred Douglas-firs stand among the slender, younger trees. We plod on, hot and sweating but content that we are making good progress up towards the high country.

Just below the bluffs forming the nose of the ridge above, we stop for a drink of water and survey the expansive upper Stein and Rutledge valleys. Leo points to where the thin ribbon of the Stein disappears — the start of the upper canyon. Closer, one thousand metres directly below us, Island Camp is barely visible, a fragile sliver of sand on the edge of the forest. On the opposite bank are the old oxbows and beaver ponds along which we hiked as we reached the valley bottom yesterday afternoon.

Scrambling up the dry, dusty bluffs under the sparse canopy of fir and pine, I am thoroughly enjoying the warmth of the mid-day sun. Sweat runs down my brow, dust clouds rise from each footprint. Gradually the firs are

Leo surveys the North Stein Valley

left behind, and gnarled whitebark pines punctuate the ridgeline. Here a long ago lightning strike ignited the resin-rich pine forest, burning the trees all across the face of the mountain. On the narrow crest of the ridge, heather meadows are dotted with the silver sculptures of fire-killed pines. The north slope drops precipitously to a brushy tributary valley streaked with long avalanche chutes.

The ridge we are on runs westward, broken by dips and knolls, but rising steadily to meet the North Stein Ridge some two kilometres away. After lunch we wander this high rooftop of the wilderness, with views all around, dipping and meandering around thickets of krummholz and up the final rock and meadow slopes to the 2,100-metre high point. The vastness of the North Stein Valley now adds to the growing panorama, encompassing the magnificent sweep of forest and peaks from the upper canyon of the Stein, past Elton and Stein lakes and unnamed tributary valleys to the distant saddle of Van Horlick Pass away to the north.

Leo breaks the silence. "Industry people are talking about putting a road through Van Horlick Pass from Highway 99 — an alternate way to haul timber out of the Stein if the Natives stop the

Elton Lake and Mount Klackarpun

proposed road through the lower canyon from Lytton because of the cultural sites there."

I ponder his statement, feeling angry that anyone would even suggest such an idea. "That's crazy, so bloody desperate! Building a logging road over an alpine pass and right through grizzly bear habitat! With all that up-hill hauling and such a long way around to the mill, I wonder if they'd even make any money. But it's probably more the principle, like making a statement — log every last valley! They got the Nahatlatch, Texas, Van Horlick, Gott, Kwoiek, Blowdown — now they want the Stein too! It's really sad that people just don't understand."

Most of society hasn't yet embraced a land ethic based on ecologically acceptable land use conduct, an ethic that recognizes the import-ance of maintaining natural functions as the very source of all life, natural wealth and pro-ductivity. An ethic based on respect and love for the natural world. We have ethics that dic-tate what is acceptable social conduct, that it is wrong to steal, hurt or kill fellow humans, be dishonest. Yet every day we rob society of its heritage and its future opportunities, accepting the loss of wildlife species and wild ecosystems as a cost of doing business. How honest are we when we cover all the atrocities and unknowns with a blind faith in our ability to "manage" and improve upon nature? Surveying the Stein from this ridge top, no calculations or eco-nomic arguments can justify any roads in this valley. It simply must remain for its own sake, just wilderness for the sake of wilderness. And I wonder if those who would see the Stein logged from their distant pedestals of political or corporate power, were they standing beside us now, would still be blind.

Turning north, we begin our long journey along the eastern divide of the North Stein. We contour down past the highest of several lakes to refill our water bottles and stop for our now customary second lunch. Leo cannot resist a swim after the hot, dusty climb out of the valley.

The last climb from the lake to the 2,400-metre peak above passes quickly. From the jumbled summit boulders, I gaze eastward into the valley of Grizzly Creek. Way down in the valley, afternoon sun slants across the treetops. A cluster of little indigo lakes lies just ahead of the advancing line of shadow cast by the peak on which we stand. The distant high ridges of Stein, Siwhe, Petlushkwohap and Skihist mountains rise from the buff-coloured rain shadow ranges. Petlushkwohap, with its curious darker rock, seems in perpetual shadow, even as the sun blazes unobstructed out of a flawless sky. Away to the north, the 8,350 Peak, a horn of broken rock named for its height in feet, keeps watch over the ridge. I wonder how we will pass this sinister looking obstacle.

The high ridge to the north — our planned route — is broken by rock towers and gullies, and an obvious line of passage is not readily discernable. The sun is already low over the western peaks, casting a shadow-etching golden glow across the mountains. Greg, who is less comfortable on steep, exposed terrain, decides to wait on the peak while Leo and I make a reconnaissance of the route ahead without our packs. I scramble down the lichen-crusted boulders.

A series of broken ledges bypass the first two peaks and intervening gullies. Leo joins me. "Think we can traverse to that far peak?" he asks. "Probably. As long as there's not a deep gully behind this pinnacle. The map isn't too useful for stuff like this. Maybe we should have stayed lower." We push on ahead, finding a passable route. Returning for our packs, Greg joins us as we carefully retrace the route, over the final broader peak, and down its northeast ridge. From a saddle in the ridge we drop

Mehatl Peak

north down a talus slope to a small icefield strewn with rocks and dirt on its lower reaches. Water flows among bedrock outcroppings and gravel moraines, and we set up camp on a heather patch beside a meltwater trickle. The sun has dropped below the ridgeline, strange lens-shaped clouds have developed and a fitful breeze ruffles the tent fly. Crowded around my candle lantern, we cook dinner, then retreat to our sleeping bags. At the end of this thirteen-hour day, I quickly fall into the deep sleep that follows physical exertion in the high country.

8,350 PEAK

With last night's wind and curious clouds, I am expecting to wake up to low cloud. But the weather is still fine, a cool, clear morning more reminiscent of fall. Today we will encounter the 8,350 Peak, an uncertain portion of the route which has been in the back of our minds since first sighting the distant dark horn from the divide at the head of Kwoiek Creek.

We traverse steep talus and heather slopes, then climb 150 metres to gain the ridge crest. The walking is easy, and the ever-present view down into the North Stein draws my eye into

North Stein Valley

the unfamiliar country to the north and east.

I am touched by the variety of the terrain here. To the east, in the headwaters of one of the many tributaries of Scudamore Creek, lies a deep blue, almost violet, oval of a lake ringed by tan-coloured scree and heather meadows. In the next valley are two entirely different little lakes, these jade green set in a bowl of pale granite talus. Every valley, ridge and meadow tells an unfolding story of natural history, of incremental geologic and ecological change on a time scale sometimes difficult to comprehend.

Further along, the ridge narrows, with the east face dropping three hundred metres to yet another lake in a deep glacier-scoured cirque. An old terminal moraine — a ridge of gravel and rock ploughed up by the snout of the one-time glacier — forms a crescent-shaped island in the shallow water.

In a saddle on the ridge I find the leg of a fawn which was devoured by a predator, perhaps a wolverine. More than a tragedy, it is a profound sign that the community of life is functioning, with its large carnivore predator-prey relationship intact.

As we traverse north, leaving the North

its beauty and wildness. The numerous large avalanche chutes, thick with herbaceous vegetation, are ideal habitat for grizzly bears, a species that requires lots of room, big wilderness.

Beyond a minor peak the gentle heather-covered ridgeline sweeps towards the eroding spire of the 8,350 Peak. As we approach, the peak looks less imposing, with detail showing on its flanks, its perceived steepness diminishing. From a bluff on its shoulder we finally have a view north around the west side of the mountain. The rugged slope is all gullies and ridges, with steep loose rock, scree and heather — impassable. We must drop four hundred metres down the west side, traversing near treeline, to bypass this peak.

Leo leads down a talus slope, around a nose of rock, and carefully kicks steps across the head of a steep dirt gully peppered with loose rocks. On the ridge beyond we descend easy heather and soft, sandy scree, then begin traversing boulder slopes, steep meadows full of marmot and pika burrows and thickets of tough krummholz. A long, ascending traverse returns us to the ridge crest two kilometres north of the 8,350 Peak. We celebrate passing this obstacle with lunch on the ridge, surveying

Camp in the meadows at the head of the south fork of Scudamore Creek

High ridge rambling, North Stein Ridge

Stein Ridge, the country changes abruptly from dry ridges of boulders to expansive meadows — big rolling basins filled with wildflowers and clumps of subalpine fir. We set up camp on a level sedge patch beside a clear brook which curves east into the Scudamore. With little talk, we each instinctively perform tasks that from long experience we know need to be done. Leo fetches water from the brook, boils it and prepares dinner while Greg and I string the food cache rope in a clump of trees at the edge of the meadow. It is a pleasant evening, and with easy walking ahead, relaxing.

CIRQUE LAKE

A curious marmot is standing upright on a giant mound, perhaps the centuries-old home of its ancestors. Its piercing whistle echoes across the basin flooded by morning sunshine. I walk gingerly toward the mound, camera ready, but the marmot detects my presence, pops down in a twist and disappears into its dwelling.

This morning brings a long walk through meadows dotted with wildflowers — lupines, daisies, cinquefoil, Indian paintbrush — over a low ridge and across the valley side to the pass at its head. From the crest of the next ridge a great basin to the northeast fills our view — long, steep, meadow-streaked slopes dotted with boulders. Beyond the far ridge, still hidden in its deep pocket, lies Cirque Lake, our destination for tonight.

We wander among the frost-broken rocks on the ridge crest, then scramble down loose talus slopes into the great basin. On a glacier-

Descending to Cirque Lake

polished ridge, its surface etched with striae, I pause to ponder the power of the ice that once was here.

A kilometre to the north we reach a cool, windy pass separating the Scudamore drainage from Van Horlick Creek to the northwest. Clouds are beginning to drag their tails across the high peaks. The cool air is welcome, though, as we climb the ridgeline rising east out of the pass. At 2,300 metres we traverse the mountainside to a low notch in the crest. One of the frequent loose boulders flips over under my boot and hurtles off down the mountain. Bounding and ricocheting down a gully and singing through the air, it shrinks until the only evidence of its continued travel is the echoing cracking and booming five hundred metres below. Thousands, millions of years of slow erosion has shaped these peaks, and my boots, like the hoof of a mountain goat or paw of a grizzly, have moved a little piece of earth as part of the process. It strikes me how harmless and innocent humans can be when stripped of technology and reduced to the simple, timeless act of self-contained travel in the wild.

From the windy little notch we gaze straight down on the blue disk of Cirque Lake a dizzying four hundred metres below. Wisps of goat hair flutter from a nearby rock. Beyond, through a pass in the Stein divide, I can see the twin incisions of the mining road to

Blowdown Pass. This is the first significant mark of human exploitation that we have seen since leaving Kwoiek Creek — otherwise there have been only a few stone route-marking cairns, the Stein trail and the cable car across the river.

From the notch we traverse east to the top of a snowfield which provides a route down to the lake. For the first time on the trip, we use our ice axes. Firmly gripping the aluminum shaft with my right hand, I reach down and swing the axe in smooth arcs, spraying cold, granular snow crystals up towards my head and arms, cutting a secure pocket into which to place my foot. A dozen such steps and I have descended the initial headwall below the moat separating snow from rock. Here the slope is shallower, about forty degrees, but the snow is firm — a slip could result in a long slide to the rocks below. I cautiously glissade down, ready to arrest a fall with my axe. As I turn to watch Leo and Greg, Leo slips and falls on his hip, accelerating rapidly. He instinctively rolls over, digging the pick of his axe and toes of his boots into the snow, applies pressure, and grinds to a stop.

Light drizzle hangs like a veil from the dark clouds scudding overhead. We amble down the gentle meadow towards the lakeshore where we are disappointed to find two fire pits — not that we didn't expect them here, only a day's travel from the Blowdown Pass road. For the moment, the feeling of remoteness, of being far from civilization, has been lessened. When our camp is set up near a little clump of subalpine fir, and the food cache strung in a grove way across the meadow, I return to the fire pits with my ice axe and bury them, scattering the blackened stones and charred wood out of sight in the fir groves.

HIGH DIVIDE

Some twenty minutes above Cirque Lake we crest the pass leading into a fork of Blowdown Creek. Here, for the first time in nearly a week, we briefly leave the Stein drainage. Contouring across loose "dinner plate" talus, we climb past three small lakes to a pass leading back into the Stein, at the head of the south fork of Cottonwood Creek. Here, a big bowl of reddish scree lies below the northeast face of Provincial Gott Peak like a martian landscape. The hollow sound of shifting stones echoes through the valley as we traverse southeast towards the far ridge crest which marks the Cottonwood-Scudamore divide.

On the divide, beside a toppled-over mineral claim post, we stop for lunch. The ridge to the east — our route — looks like a series of narrow rock peaks, despite the complete absence of such features on the topographical map. The next hour is spent dealing with this mapping error — scrambling up and down over the ridge crest, straddling wedge-shaped rock spines and following ledges and gullies through a maze of krummholz. Each peak that seems like the last is followed by another, but the joy and exhilaration of high scrambling in this airy place — deliberately and methodically placing feet and hands, seeking out cracks and ledges, grasping the cold, abrasive rock — compensates for the extra physical effort of the climb.

After the final peak the ridge drops in a long gentle curve to a forested saddle, then rises again to the high peaks above Silver Queen Mine. Meadows along the crest become increasingly dotted with conical Engelmann spruce and rounded whitebark pines. The ground cover is sparser, with scattered clumps of grasses replacing the carpet of heather, reflecting the drier rain shadow climate. To the north the scar of the mining road slashes diagonally across the otherwise pristine forested wall of Cottonwood Creek valley. But to the south there are no scars to be seen; the long sweeping curve of forest-carpeted Scudamore Creek valley emerges from the dark peaks near Cirque Lake. Near the saddle we settle down on the dry pine-needled ground beneath a grove of trees and enjoy a snack while waiting out a passing squall.

Shafts of sunlight slant through the brood-

Thunderstorm over Scudamore Creek

ing thunderheads at the head of Scudamore Creek, illuminating the off and on rain squalls like spotlight beams. The distant glacier-polished slabs of rain-soaked rock scintillate in the sun. The last squall passes, and crisp shadows define the ridges, trees, and glacier-scoured basins. We are reluctant to leave this high and lovely ridge, where perfect tent sites nestle behind a wall of wind-whipped pine trees. But there is no water, so we must drop two hundred metres down the north side of the ridge to a small lake.

Throughout the two basins, bulldozer tracks and diggings mark the Silver Queen's mining activity. For all the mess in this beautiful high country, for the roads slashed across Cottonwood and Blowdown valleys, this is only a hobby mine for a few prospectors. It has never provided steady employment, or real wealth; it has only succeeded in diminishing the wildness of this special place.

From our camp in the woods near the little lake, we can see none of the mess. Darkness falls quickly over the shady basin under leaden skies. Tomorrow we will follow the Angel's Walk to the Stein River.

ANGEL'S WALK

I did not know the late Father Damasus Payne, but I do know why he called this high ridge the Angel's Walk. From the narrow stony crest, long slopes drop on either side to the roaring vastness of Scudamore and Cottonwood creek valleys. High and fresh and windy, it feels like heaven on earth.

Once our morning legs were accustomed to the physical activity, the steady two-hundred-metre climb up the steep bowl to the crest had gone quickly, and now we ramble along the ridge among stunted pines and spruce krummholz. Every now and then, we see ancient pines hacked and squared into mineral claim posts, not so subtle reminders of the fragility of this wilderness.

The fascinatingly twisted ridge dips and rises in a series of saddles and knolls. In a few places we must scramble across the sidehills, edging our feet into the sandy scree, to avoid crags and bluffs. After an hour we reach a high point and stop for a snack near the bleached skull of a goat. Vestiges of a trail lead over the next knoll, and along a series of dry meadows lined by fire-killed whitebark pines. Then the ridge drops off towards the Stein, which meanders over one thousand metres below. Leo traces the river's course into the hazy distance towards Lytton. Far below to the east Cottonwood Creek roars through its deepening canyon. As we emerge onto the nose of the ridge in bright sunshine, overlooking the Stein

Scudamore Creek valley

Valley, I can feel the dryness in the air.

Squat Douglas-fir and skeletons of dead ponderosa pine punctuate the steep, dusty ridge. We drop rapidly down until, quite suddenly, a high cliff blocks the route. After shouting a warning to Greg and Leo, who are slightly behind, I begin gingerly working my way east across bluffs and loose, dry soil to a gap between cliffs. Wedging my boot toes into a corner, I grasp a sturdy fir root and cautiously climb down the gully. An awkward spot forces me to remove my pack and lower it by rope to the next ledge. I repeat the lowering procedure down the next bluff to where Greg and Leo are waiting, having managed to drop down earlier and bypass the steep section.

Towering thunderheads are rapidly building as the hot, dry mid-day air collides with cool air over the mountains. The crackling-dry forest is criss-crossed with animal trails and cast with the peculiar yellowish glow, hushed stillness and faint presence of electric energy that precedes a thunder storm. The broad crowns of ponderosa pines — symbolic of the dry interior — start to sway as the wind rushes from hot air to cool. With the first crack and rumble of thunder, heavy rain drops begin to fall, and we take shelter in a grove to put on rain gear. The thunder shower soon passes, though, and we find a nice lunch spot on a dry rock padded with lichen and pine needles.

Below the lunch rock I stop to examine several ponderosa pines that have been badly burned on the uphill side. In this hillside location debris piles up against the uphill side of the tree trunks. During forest fires this debris burns long and hot, sometimes consuming half the width of the tree trunk. But the hardy pines have responded by beginning a slow healing process, covering the scars with lobes of accelerated growth.

A final steeper section brings us to the valley bottom where pleasant Douglas-fir and pine woods are interspersed with rocky clearings covered by moss and lichen. "Red tag!" Greg announces, pointing at a fluorescent orange

trail marker on a tree — we have reached the Stein Valley trail, ending the cross country portion of our trek.

SEVEN THOUSAND YEARS

The Lytton and Mount Currie people have used the Stein for over seven thousand years, leaving only minimal signs of their presence, viewing the land as a functioning, interrelated system where each part benefits the whole. In the quiet woods beside the milky green river, just upstream from Cottonwood Creek, is the Rediscovery Camp. Here traditional Native values, respect for the land and the sustenance it provides, and wilderness skills are passed on to

Evening, Cottonwood Falls

Bark-stripped cedar tree

Native and non-Native children. Here, too, foresters from logging company Fletcher Challenge had planned their first clearcut.

Leo worked for Rediscovery one summer, and we are welcomed warmly by the staff and elders in the camp. We have also arrived on the night of a feast and are invited to stay for dinner — a gesture greatly appreciated after a week of simple backpacking foods.

Down by the river beside a big fire, one of the elders points out the salmon in the river, and describes how the fresh fish now dressed on the banquet table were caught with a long barbed pole, its tip hand-fashioned from metal and hardwood. When we reluctantly leave after the feast and walk down the twilight trail to Cottonwood Creek, we are pleasantly filled with good food and good memories of a short time spent with a culture that gives nature the respect it deserves.

Leo and I wander up to nearby Cottonwood Falls, climbing a bluff above the cascades, and silently gaze out over the Stein Valley. Far to the west snowy peaks near Elton Lake hold on to the last colour of the sun streaming through broken clouds.

MARKINGS

The morning begins with the unusual pleasure of a relaxed stroll down the well-worn trail winding among lichen-dappled boulders and pine trees. The dry woods gradually merge into thickets of aspen and then into dense coniferous forest punctuated by large fire-blackened Douglas-firs. The sight of claw marks on some of the aspen trunks reminds us that just a few days ago one of the staff at the Rediscovery Camp had seen a big grizzly bear here.

We walk on through the ever-changing forest to Burnt Cabin Creek, then on towards Ponderosa Creek. Groves of cedars form cool, damp interludes in the dry forest, and thickets of aspen, cottonwood and birch line the edges of beaver ponds on the river bottomlands. Where the trail passes close to the banks of the Stein there is the strong smell of dead fish; bears have been feeding here. We pass quickly in case the animals are still in the area, noting the fresh carcass of a large steelhead lying in the rushes.

At Ponderosa Creek shelter we stop for lunch beside the river. With only a day and a half of easy hiking left, we sort through our remaining food. Leo, who has more food left, bargains with Greg and I who are running short. Desirable items such as trail mix and granola bars command high prices, but little comes of the bartering.

We have all walked this trail before, and our familiarity with its features makes it like an old friend. The damp cottonwood flats along the river, the dry rocks of Snake Bluffs, the big firs, the aspen groves, are all pleasant land-

Early morning along the Stein River

marks along the trail. Near the cable car across the Stein, Leo points out a cedar stripped of bark for baskets by natives nearly a century ago. On the cracking face of the scar are primitive paintings of animals and humans lightly crusted with lichen.

A short way beyond, across the Stein, stands Klein's Cabin, an oddly constructed building with wide spaces between the logs, more like a corral fence than a weatherproof shelter. It was built in 1953 by trapper Adam Klein and his son. Klein envisioned a road and tourist resort in the heart of the valley. The Native spiritual values notwithstanding, his vision was perhaps ahead of its time, seeing the wilderness scenery as something to be used and valued in its own right.

We cross the river in the little aluminum

basket of the cable car. Downstream we pass Earl's Cabin, a reconstruction of a cabin originally built by Fred Earl, another early trapper and prospector who is said to have taken $12,000 worth of gold from Earl Creek. Downstream, at Teaspoon Creek, Natives long ago stripped bark from cedar trees to weave clothing and baskets. I am saddened to see some of the historic scars vandalized by initial-carvers.

The Stein roars through the narrowing valley among big boulders. We press on for another forty minutes to a pleasant campsite beside the river, not far from the start of the lower canyon. This will be our last night in the Stein. Off in the shadows beside the steep wall of the valley an elusive animal darts across our field of view. Its low-slung shape suggests a marten or fisher, but it seemed larger. The mystery remains unsolved as twilight falls over the river.

On our last morning we eat breakfast at a relaxed pace. Leo sits for a long time by the river with the maps, calculating the distance we have travelled. Then he walks up to camp and announces the results. "By tonight, we'll have walked ninety-two kilometres in ten days, climbed 6,860 metres, and descended 7,960 metres." We all feel fit and relaxed as we casually pack up our last camp.

The dusty trail winds on into the lower canyon of the Stein. Below, the river races urgently, just as it has for thousands of years. In the heart of the canyon is a rock bluff, a place known by the Natives as *ts'ets'ekw'*, which means "markings." Along the base of the cliffs are nearly two hundred Native pictographs, mysterious ochre paintings depicting animals and people in primitive style. The pictographs are of great spiritual significance — one more signature of the Native culture that has held a presence in the Stein for thousands of years. In the dry woods above the bluff, where lichen-crusted pines and a solitary juniper cling to the boulders, fading survey ribbons mark the route of the proposed logging road. I can visualize the destruction that would be caused by pushing this road through the sacred canyon. The booming of dynamite blasts echoing off the walls as boulders tumbled down upon the ancient paintings. The writing on the walls of this natural shrine vanishing in the splitting of stone and cordite-scented air. Another valley forever changed. The wildness and the history lost.

From the canyon, the Stein flows only a few more kilometres to where its milky blue-green waters merge with the chocolate-coloured Fraser. We slowly climb the last rise to the trailhead. As always at the end of a long trip, there is a mixture of excitement and sadness, for while our goal has been reached, we are also leaving the purity and simplicity of the wilderness to return to the faster pace of city life. It is all brought into clear perspective a half-hour later. A house trailer has become jammed on the highway bridge over the Thompson River in Lytton. Local people heading for work wait, some impatiently. An overweight woman tests the temper of a man hard at work trying to free the trailer from the bridge railing. It is hot. There is anger. The patience of the wilderness is not here. I glance at the Stein River valley across the Fraser, and the view takes me back into the aspen groves and needle-carpeted glens along the swirling river.

$\mathcal{K}$YUQUOT

RAINFOREST BY THE SEA

Great swells roll in endlessly from the open Pacific, their peaks raked by the stiff westerly wind, blowing salty spray into our faces. Our tiny Achilles inflatable rides up their sides, hangs suspended for a second, then slams down onto the next wave. Again and again, we are showered with briny water as the outboard labours against the big seas and the hypalon rubber skin resounds like a beaten drum. All around us, the biggest ocean on earth tosses and turns and rolls in an unending dance. Ian Mackenzie squints into the low sun and salt spray as he pilots the boat northwest from the

tiny fishing village of Kyuquot on the outer northwest coast of Vancouver Island. When we have pushed out beyond the deadly surf-swept rocks, he veers the boat around and we skim parallel to the swells, riding their long backs up and down.

The rainforest along the shore, illuminated golden-green by the afternoon sunlight, forms a rolling carpet across the coastal plain. But beyond, on the slopes of Saint Paul's Dome and neighbouring Mount Paxton, the rainforest is gone. Sparse new growth, mostly the weeds of spring, colours the slopes a greenish hue, but

Brooks Peninsula

the blackened stumps and eroding soil are the unmistakable signatures of clearcut logging. The logging extends five hundred vertical metres from the ridge top right down to the waterline where Native burial caves echo with the crashing of the sea.

We pitch and roll gently in the shelter of the tiny Barrier Islands viewing the spectacle that has become a symbol of what is happening to the northwest coast of Vancouver Island. A symbol so powerful that it graced the pages of *National Geographic*. With each passing year the line of wilderness is pushed further back towards the storm-raked Brooks Peninsula.

Ian Mackenzie, Clinton Webb and I have come here to experience, photograph and document what remains of the wildest side of Vancouver Island. Ian is a wilderness photographer whose personal mission is to photograph threatened wilderness areas to raise public awareness. When not exploring British Columbia's wilderness, he literally risks life and limb tramping through the jungles of distant Malaysia, armed with cameras and video equipment, recording the appalling injustices brought on the Native people there by clearcut logging of their tropical rainforest homelands.

Clinton, my friend and colleague in environmental work, is a stickler for accuracy and one of the most tenacious conservationists I know. When pried away from his work, he is an equally tenacious bushwhacker, as I know from the Megin adventure we shared two years ago.

Surrounding the Brooks Peninsula are a handful of largely undisturbed river valleys: the Klaskish, East, Nasparti, Battle and Power. Over the next ten days we plan to explore the latter three, and the mysteries of the wilderness coastline in between.

Ian's versatile inflatable boat allows us to travel fast with bulky gear and photo equipment. While lacking the elegant, self-propelled simplicity of ocean kayaks — the ideal mode of travel on this coastline — using the motor boat will leave maximum time for hiking up the rainforest valleys where few people other than timber cruisers have ventured.

We had launched this June morning at Fair Harbour, a desolate parking lot and government wharf that are all that remain of a one-time forest industry community on Kyuquot Sound, 150 kilometres west of Campbell River. When the local forest was exhausted, the camp moved across the inlet to continue the onslaught. Racing across Kyuquot Sound we passed eagle nest trees standing isolated on logged coastlines, and rounded appropriately named Surprise Island, stripped of forest from shore to shore. Nearby, a lean black bear upturned stones on the beach in search of crabs.

In Kyuquot, Tom Pater, a teacher and one of the key people in KEEPS — Kyuquot Environmental and Economic Protection Society — had met us on the wharf. Tall, bearded and soft spoken, Tom ushered us towards his house.

"When I saw the little skiff come into the cove, I knew it was you," he said. "C'mon in, I've put some tea on. Sam will be here in a little while."

We spent the pleasant, sunny afternoon with Tom and Sam Kayra, learning about the Kyuquot wilderness from these concerned people who have tirelessly fought to protect their surroundings from the unending tide of clearcut logging

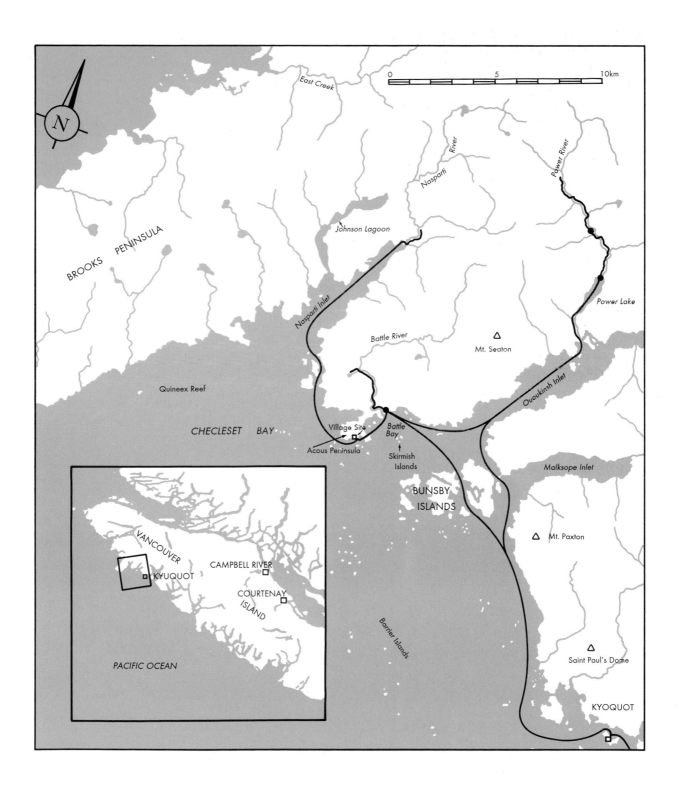

East Creek

Nasparti River

Power River

Johnson Lagoon

BROOKS PENINSULA

Nasparti Inlet

Power Lake

Battle River

Mt. Seaton

Quineex Reef

Ououkinsh Inlet

CHECLESET BAY

Village Site

Battle Bay

Acous Peninsula

Skirmish Islands

Malksope Inlet

BUNSBY ISLANDS

Mt. Paxton

Barrier Islands

Saint Paul's Dome

KYOQUOT

VANCOUVER

KYUQUOT

CAMPBELL RIVER

COURTENAY ISLAND

PACIFIC OCEAN

0   5   10km

by multinational corporations. Yet despite their efforts, clearcutting of ancient rainforests has continued to the point where only a few large areas remain intact. When the seas calmed a little in the afternoon and it became time for us to leave, Tom had treated us like old friends.

"Are you sure you won't spend the night? It's rough out there and you've only got a little skiff. You're welcome to stay at the cove tonight. You could leave first thing in the morning."

But we were eager to be on our way and soon waved goodbye to our new-found friends. "Be sure to drop in on your return," said Tom, smiling and waving from the dock, no doubt wishing that he could join us. With that we left the shelter of Walters Island and headed out into the swells.

Loading the boat, Fair Harbour

Soon we are skimming across the waves again towards the sheltered waters of the Bunsby Islands. A sea otter poked its head up through a kelp bed, as if to welcome us, then disappeared into the inky sea.

Sea otters had been heavily hunted for their rich pelts, to the point where they were eliminated from the west coast of Vancouver Island by the early 1900s. A landmark four-year conservation project beginning in 1969 saw eighty-nine otters re-introduced to the Kyuquot area from Amchitka Island and Prince William Sound in Alaska. With abundant food supplies, including shellfish and sea urchins, the population has flourished to about five hundred animals.

The late sun hangs low as we creep into the long shadow of the Brooks Peninsula. In the mauve light of evening we skim through the rock-lined passages on rippled seas. Ahead no logging mars the mountains above Checleset Bay. We are here. The superlative west coast wilderness surrounding the Brooks; the ancient rainforests of the Nasparti and Power rivers, the Native village site on the Acous Peninsula and the long curve of Battle Bay Beach will be our home in the days ahead.

Ian cuts the engine and the little rubber boat glides up on the sand in the mouth of the Battle River. We unload gear and set up camp on the beach, then cook dinner sitting around a little driftwood fire. Thousands of years ago, the Nuu-chah-nulth Natives may have done the same.

BATTLE BAY

The names in this area, Battle Bay and the Skirmish Islands, commemorate the battles between the Nuu-chah-nulth, formerly known as the Nootka, and the Kwakiutl to the north. The rugged Brooks Peninsula, defiantly jutting out to sea, was the boundary of their traditional territories, a line which undoubtedly fluctuated from time to time.

It is remarkably calm for the west coast this morning. Hardly a swell interrupts the rippled water of Battle Bay. We busy ourselves prepar-

ing gear for today's exploration up Battle River and rigging a cache for the remaining food in a gnarled spruce along the beach.

Ian unpacks two small inflatable kayaks, which he calls "rubber duckies," for paddling up the rivers. Clinton inflates one of the boats and carries it over to the bank of the Battle River, eager to try it out on today's exploration. The little craft seems incredibly unstable, wobbling and rotating under us, spinning around at the slightest paddle stroke. We struggle just to stay upright. As we almost capsize, our predicament suddenly seems very silly, and we begin to laugh. The giggling turns into uncontrollable convulsions, leaving us paralysed, unable to speak and gasping for air, bobbing in the Battle River! Then Clinton manages to escape. Catching his breath, he announces, "Let's walk! I'm not getting in that thing again!" We tie the silly yellow boat to a log

and walk up the river in our rubber boots. Ian has paddled and waded upstream in his chestwaders, unaware of our performance.

At first, the coastal influence of wind and salt spray keeps the forest dominantly Sitka spruce of moderate height. Unlike other coniferous trees, the spruce is able to tolerate the salt spray of the outer coast. In fact, the magnesium in the ocean spray is beneficial to these trees. From Alaska all the way down to northern California an almost continuous fringe of Sitka spruce, trimmed to wedge shape by the salty prevailing winds, lines the coast.

As we push upstream, the trees become less stunted and the trunks stretch out towards the sky. Log jams and the debris of winter floods block the channel. Rotting leaves and twigs, trapped behind the logs, begin their gradual transformation into forest soil, held in place by the fine roots of new alders. The clean gravel clicks beneath our boots. Fern-studded glens and majestic spruce groves thrive on the deep, alluvial soil along the creek. Further back, twisted cedars spiral upwards from swollen bases up to four metres in diameter. A few kilometres upstream, the character of the creek changes from gravel beds to boulders the size of soccer balls. A long reach stretches straight into the sun, and the babbling waters scintillate in its radiance. Great spike-topped cedars lean out from the banks. Animal trails

Sitka spruce cones

Nasparti River

tunnel through the heavy growth of salal and salmonberry. We slosh on to a sharp bend.

Clinton and I decide to head up a tributary to a small lake. Ian is behind, photographing the forest, so the two of us head into the tall forest of spruce and hemlock. The ground is uneven, with low-lying patches of skunk cabbage and salmonberry. Some of this area is poorly drained, a seemingly impenetrable tangle of fallen trees and undergrowth suspended in a latticework of logs above the saturated ground. With no fires to consume forest debris, all that falls to earth remains here until it decomposes back into the soil. A great recycling machine, but not a place for efficient travel by clumsy bipeds.

The shore of the little lake is even more tangled; layers of sphagnum moss and debris build up a centuries-old organic layer which gradually supports more and more plant life. A few more centuries and this shallow lake will become a marsh, and then finally be reclaimed by the forest.

A beaver paddles patiently across the mirror-calm water. We feel that we are witnessing a simple timeless routine of the wilderness. Then with a loud slap of its tail and the churning of water the beaver is gone. Perhaps it was our scent.

We crash back down to the Battle River, then follow its winding course back towards the beach. Around the last few bends the smell of salty sea air permeates the forest. The golden light of the declining sun climbs up towards the treetops, leaving the creek bed in shadow.

NASPARTI

It is another warm clear morning on the

Battle River

sand of Battle Bay Beach. Tiny waves gently lick the cobbles. Ian is already down on the beach readying the boat for the trip around the Acous Peninsula to the Nasparti River. A couple of jerry cans of gas, rain gear, food, and camera equipment is loaded. Soon the red inflatable is racing among the offshore islets around the Acous. The Brooks Peninsula comes into view, its sawtooth spine missed by the last ice age, home to disjunct species of lichen and liverwort. We pull up on a small cobble beach to photograph the views of Nasparti Inlet and the Brooks.

Nasparti Inlet faces out to sea and a light chop has developed. Here and there along the inlet, the logging scars of small business sales mar the otherwise pristine landscape. In the early 1970s, someone even went into neighbouring Johnson Lagoon, as pretty as a south sea atoll, and grubbed out the good timber along the shore. Little creek gullies, where the big trees grew, are scraped of their forest. Around the last bend of the inlet, the scars disappear, and the pristine estuary of the Nasparti River lies ahead, a sliver of pale green set against a backdrop of lofty Sitka spruce trees and forested mountains.

The river itself is too shallow for the outboard, so we circle around to the north side of the estuary where a tiny sand beach offers a good landing site. Drifting in, an osprey wheels overhead, dives abruptly to splash the water, then flies off with a fish in its talons. Ian inflates one of the kayaks for the return trip from the river mouth. "The tide will be up in a few hours," he says, "flooding the tidal flats that we'll walk across to reach the river. We'll

The record-sized Sitka spruce

moth bell-bottomed trunk of an immense Sitka spruce rises to a broad crown of drooping branches. At sixty metres, it is not tall by spruce standards, but this is the largest living Sitka yet recorded in British Columbia by a combination of circumference, height and crown spread. Loggers talk of bigger trees, then show postcards of the butt log on a logging truck, dead after seven-hundred years in the ancient forest. This tree is alive. Its life began atop a long-rotted log, and the spreading roots still outline the shape; twenty metres around the base, nearly fourteen metres around the trunk at breast height above the estimated germination point on the log that no longer exists. The crown spans some twenty-seven metres, shading out the understorey. Another spruce nearby is nearly twelve metres around at breast height, a third is ten metres. All throughout the grove are these great trees, monuments to the richness of this ecosystem.

We saunter among the fat, moss-sheathed boles back towards the estuary. Golden light streams in from the forest edge. With the tide up, the sedge meadows are flooded. Ian and I paddle the little yellow kayak to retrieve the boat. We then motor slowly up the river channel, now deep with the high tide, picking up Clinton and nosing in to the opposite bank. Ian knows of a special place.

The grove is open, grassy underfoot. Bears sometimes play here beneath the pot-bellied, fairy-tale-like spruce trees that bristle with moss- and fern-padded branches. Everything appears to have been perfectly placed; each tree, fern clump and grassy glade. "Isn't this magical?" asks Ian, obviously enchanted by this place. "Of all the spruce groves I've seen in estuaries up and down the coast, I think this is the most wonderful. When we came here last year, there were bears rolling around in the grass, just playing."

Wisps of cloud are now tinged crimson over the Brooks. The peninsula lies as a great dark shadow, a formidable breakwater sheltering us from the Pacific vastness. In the twilight we skim out of Nasparti Inlet, skipping across the crests

need the rubber duckie to retrieve the boat."

Sedges hiss quietly in the breeze and tickle my legs as I wander across the flats to the river. In the forest beyond, the same breeze keeps the no-see-ums at bay. Overhead the golden-green moss-padded limbs of the spruce trees glow in the sunshine. All around great symmetrical boles, bristling with branches like giant bottle brushes, rise from the grassy, fern-studded forest floor. The grove continues for a long way, pure spruce. Then a salmonberry thicket interrupts the easy going.

THE GIANTS

In an open grove, not far from the gently swirling waters of the Nasparti River, the mam-

like a child's stone on a millpond. Rounding the Acous Peninsula, we glide back into Battle Bay, pulling up in the mouth of the river. The ragged crowns of the windblown spruce trees are silhouetted against the fading pink. Our little driftwood fire burns again. After dinner, the gentle murmur of the lapping sea closes the curtains on another wonderful day among the giants.

FORGOTTEN CITY

In the brilliant morning sun we pack our camp on Battle Bay Beach and load the gear into the boat. Our plan for the day is to cruise up Ououkinsh Inlet to the Power River. The forest service is considering allowing a road to be punched up the Power to salvage-log blowdown from a storm last December. We know that the real motive is to get a road into yet another largely unlogged valley, a foot in the door for the logging industry.

But first, we will look for a forgotten city.

So calm and brilliant a day is rare on this coast renowned for its fury. We cruise slowly along between the rocks off Acous Peninsula, scanning the shore for clues to the old native village site. Behind a small gravel beach that looks like the perfect landing for a great cedar canoe, the forest appears younger, less craggy. A solitary, silvered cedar pole rises out of the greenery like a leaning flag pole. We pull up in the little cove and walk into the shoreline fringe of bush. We have found the village. The wolf and sea otter still stare out to sea from the weathered welcoming pole, mossy with shoots of salal growing from cracks and ledges. Here and there, a touch of subtle blue paint hints at the original colouring. The telltale U-notched posts of the longhouse lean at giddy angles; one is propped up against the side of the pole. Nearby is a fallen pole, face down in the rainforest, with a spruce perhaps seventy or eighty years old growing on its back.

All around is an incredible sense of history. The scattered rotting posts and planks and sea shells connect us to a distant time. From the grassy knoll above that served as a lookout, we gaze out at the same rocks and surf and islands that the Nuu-chah-nulth did for centuries. We spend a long time exploring the site, photographing the poles and contemplating the bustle of life that once was here. A group of kayakers paddles by, unaware of the significance of the little crescent of gravel beach that once sheltered the great cedar canoes. We leave everything as we found it, taking with us only photographs and memories.

At mid-day we cruise up Ououkinsh Inlet, skipping over the lightly chopped seas. The high, pristine forested slopes of Mount Seaton rise behind Battle Bay. The Bunsbys lie to the west like a fleet of anchored ships. The air is fresh and breezy and the sea sparkles; a day

Welcoming pole, Acous Peninsula

Returning to the earth, Acous Peninsula

when the wilderness makes you feel vibrant and alive.

Just beyond the Bunsbys, near Izard Point, a small lagoon lies sheltered in the lee of a low island. Twisted cedars, shore pines and a few windblown Douglas-fir line the rocky shore above the clear blue-green water. But behind the fringe of shoreline trees are the silvered stumps and eroded slopes of a clearcut mountainside. The few who see this place will not be fooled by the facade along the shore.

POWER RIVER

We set off up the inlet again, soon dodging between the Hisnit Islands near the mouth of the Power River. From where we drift in the lee of the islands, the Power valley is visible, stretching as a green-carpeted defile into the mountains. Overhead, a single massive, billowing cumulus cloud hovers, as if to isolate this one valley. Ian deftly pilots the inflatable through a narrow rock-lined passage into the river mouth. A compact estuary, backed by lichen-crusted Sitka spruces, occupies the shoreline between the river and an adjacent island.

There is the gentle hiss of the sedges on the pontoons as we nose into the shore through a shallow tidal passage. Ian checks the tide tables. "It's almost high tide now. We'll want to leave here at high tide to get out of the estuary. That means we should plan to be back here on Sunday morning, around eleven." With that knowledge, we unload our gear and pull the boat up above the tideline, lashing it to a beached log. Food and gear is sorted and the surplus cached, hanging in a spruce tree. Ian inflates the two kayaks. To Clinton's and my relief, the rubber duckies handle much better when stabilized by heavy loads, and our little yellow fleet sets sail up into the mouth of the Power.

A kilometre of bouldery river bed separates the river mouth from Power Lake, so we must pack the gear and boats upstream. Two trips each and all the gear is at the lake.

The lake outlet is a narrow cleft in the rocks, lined by cliffs hung with delicate maidenhair ferns and clumps of salal. Tiny pockets of wildflowers bloom in moist places near the shore. The water in the passage is glass calm, and its inky surface mirrors the steep forested shoreline of Power Lake. Ian paddles off up the lake, his one-man paddling causing the boat to oscillate back and forth in a comical way. Clinton and I follow. Just then, a large fish bursts from the placid water, jumping for insects flying low over the water, startling us as we glide out onto the rippled surface. At the far end of the lake, we can see the dark, conical shapes of giant spruce trees beside the white sliver of gravel that marks the river mouth. A half-hour later we pull up near a sandy campsite, obviously used before, probably by fishermen.

On the steep, rocky bluffs above the head of the lake is one of the blowdown patches mentioned in the forestry report — merely one phase in the timeless cycle of the natural forest. Elsewhere we can see old blowdown patches that are now covered with healthy young trees. Left alone, nature will heal itself.

Over our evening campfire we discuss plans for the days ahead. "If we take food for three days, we can camp a day's hike up the valley and explore further from there," Ian suggests. "I'd like to try and photograph some elk." "Could we get to the top of this mountain in a day from there?" asks Clinton, pointing to

Ian's proposed campsite on the map. "If the weather's good, I'd sure like to get a view and some photos of the valley from above. Can you imagine? Totally pristine forest! Right from ridge top to ridge top!" "I think we'd get a wonderful view, but we may have to stay up there a night to get the right lighting," adds Ian, as always carefully considering the photographic conditions. We decide to pack three days' food and let the weather decide the exact plan.

The local Natives from Kyuquot village have cut a rough trail up the lower valley to the second blowdown patch which is part of the salvage-logging proposal. From their camp just back from the shore, the trail winds through cool alder thickets and clusters of mammoth, moss-sheathed Sitka spruce, then passes through an area handlogged in the Second World War for "airplane spruce." The wood of the Sitka spruce is light and strong, and was prized for its excellence in aircraft construction before the widespread use of metal alloys. The trees in this valley must have been exceptionally fine, for fifty years ago this was remote country indeed for a logger to venture. The mossy stumps have springboard notches in their sides, where the early loggers inserted planks to reach above the wide-spreading bases. Standing among the alders, these monuments are capped with mops of young hemlock trees growing in their rich rotting wood. For a long way up the valley, these subtle signs of civilization stand here and there in the rainforest.

Near a bend in the river, where a clear pool is overhung by ferns and towering spruce, tons of gravel and debris has been flooded into the forest. Great spruce boles, some seventy metres long, lie crisscrossed. I imagine the fury of a winter night when the rain streamed down ceaselessly and the swollen, sediment-laden river burst its banks and ran wild through this ancient forest. The splintering of spruce, ripping, tearing and crashing to earth; what a sight and sound it must have been! The remaining standing trees form a sparse, scruffy overhead canopy of broken limbs that echoes the violence of the event. But

Sitka spruce, Power River valley

now warm sun streams through the open stand among the flood-scarred trunks. We select a smooth gravel bar amid the natural devastation as our campsite.

ELK TRACKS

Low morning cloud scuttles any plans for a climb to the ridge top for a view. Instead, we set off upstream past the flooded area. Last winter's blowdown is evident along the valley side, and in one flat along the river. Hundreds of trees are uprooted or snapped off, but it is not the scene of unparalleled devastation suggested in the forestry reports. Clinton, a forest technician by trade, notes the many living trees still standing within the blowdown. Vigorous natural regeneration will quickly fill the gaps. In fact, blowdown patches and the resulting gaps in the overhead canopy of branches are the driving force of forest succession in the temperate rainforest. The shade-tolerant seedlings hidden in the depths of the forest wait for just such an opening to race upwards into the light.

A wide gravel bar sweeps to the right along a reach of the river channel, then ends abruptly at a rock bluff where a big hemlock has toppled across the river. We cross to the opposite bank and follow an elk trail into a magnificent forest of tall hemlock. Scattered among the hemlocks are enormous Sitka spruce, rising like moss-padded columns. The ground is often open, for elk have browsed here. In fact, the Power valley has one of the highest density Roosevelt elk populations remaining on Vancouver Island. Fifteen to twenty animals, perhaps more, are thought to travel between the Power and Nasparti valleys through a low pass in the headwaters, but surveys are sketchy and little is known about the wildlife in these valleys. On the sandbars, sidehills, valley bottom — literally everywhere we have walked — there are signs of elk.

With Clinton and Ian absorbed in their photography, I soon find myself alone in the great forest.

"Airplane spruce" logging: memories of the war years

Gazing straight up a seventy-metre spruce, my mind's image soars beyond the treetops, over hills and valleys and a million ancient, living, transpiring trees, mentally tracing and measuring the distance to civilization. Engulfed by the dense, verdant, sound-dampening forest of conifers, and physically isolated from any communities by the incisions of coastal inlets, a special quality pervades the landscape — a heightened sense of wildness, a mystical, emotionally stirring power accentuated by the closed-in, canyon-like aspect of the valley. I wander from one giant spruce to the next, from riverside clusters and groves to solitary, scaly-barked giants deep among the hemlocks. On the forest floor are the heart-shaped leaves of false lily-of-the-valley, the delicate five-fingered fronds of maidenhair ferns, and sweeps of deep-green sword fern. The occasional alder tree stands draped with moss in a salmonberry thicket like a cypress in a Louisiana bayou.

Overhead is a green latticework of overlapping branches, thickly padded with moss. Entire communities of insects spend their life cycles in this upper forest canopy, a world of its own as inaccessible and mysterious as the ocean floor. The comparison reminds me that a tiny diving seabird, the marbled murrelet, nests on the wide moss-padded limbs of the rainforest trees. Each morning at dawn during spring and early summer, hundreds of murrelets fly up the coastal valleys from their offshore feeding areas to their elusive ancient forest nests. Only a few nests have been found in Canada. I wonder how many others lie in the slash after logging, and how long this threatened species will survive in the face of the elimination of its habitat.

One of the big spruces stands squarely in the centre of a natural debris slide where rocks and mud have flowed around its base, but the tree seems unaffected. All around, I am surprised to see spruce seedlings in the forest, for usually they are shaded out by more shade-tolerant trees and shrubs. Perhaps the browsing of the elk here, which keeps the underbrush

Power River rainforest

down, allows the spruce to regenerate. As the valley side steepens, the forest changes to mostly hemlock.

The elk trail dips across little stream gullies, where I can feel the flow of cool damp air, then tunnels through dense huckleberry thickets. Needles and leaves brush off the branches and down my shirt collar, itching on my sweaty back. The path twists up across a bluff above a clear pool, then drops to a pretty little spruce grove — a perfect mossy, fern-studded flat beside the river. I settle on the narrow gravel beach bordering the pool, watching the clear waters bubble around the bend beneath the bluff. Sitting quietly, my shoulders unconsciously drop and I feel the ebb of stress from my pack-burdened muscles as I enter the gentle rhythm of nature. Not looking at things, but

sensing — being absorbed by the completeness of the place, the balance of interactions between water and stone, between nodding fronds of ferns and cool, damp, forest-scented breezes, between the quiet, fluid melody of moving water and delicate percussion of dripping rivulets. In this balance I find a wonderful feeling of serenity, a sense of peace.

A short distance upstream, I cross the Power on a fallen tree and find another idyllic little spruce grove on the opposite bank. Clusters of big spruce stand between open, park-like glades. The understorey is neatly browsed by elk, and another well-worn trail winds upstream into mossy hemlock forest. I wander on through the greenery, dropping onto the gravel bar where the river splits into numerous channels, and pushing into a dense

Ian at work (Clinton Webb)

cathedral-like forest. The standing trees are massive — two, three and even four metres thick — with big bell-bottomed bases. Some rise tall, straight and limb-less; others are squat, lumpy-trunked, twisted and branchy. When a couple of hand-loggers walked into this grove fifty years ago and with a trained eye carefully picked the finest, straightest-grained trunks for aircraft wood, theirs must have been a sense of pride. The forest left behind was still alive and magnificent. I am thankful for what they left. Today decisions about what to take and what to leave seem to be made after the trees are already dead on the ground.

BACK TO THE SEA

Our time in the wilderness is coming to a close. We pack up our gear one more time in the big waterproof dry bags, load the rubber duckies, and paddle off down Power Lake toward the rock portal at its outlet. On the portage down the river to the estuary, Ian sees a big black bear ambling out on the rocks. Our presence scares it into the undergrowth, but it is good to have met one of the local inhabitants. This valley, this wilderness, belongs to the bears and salmon and elk and thousands of other life forms. It is their home — we are only visitors.

A mottled sky of mixed sun and cloud hangs over Ououkinsh Inlet as we race out towards the open sea. Banking left, we skim through the narrow passage past a crumbling cabin on the Upsowis Indian reserve to the mouth of Malksope Inlet. The steep sides of this inlet are heavily scarred by massive soil erosion from clearcut logging. In places, even twenty years have not greened-up the barren talus slides. We turn away from the depressing view and nose into a cove near the mouth of an unnamed, unlogged little creek drainage. There is a wonderful coastal forest here, with wind-blown Douglas-fir and Sitka spruce along the salal-lined streambed. We soak up a last dose of west coast wilderness in these sun-dappled woods beside the silver sea. Back behind

salmonberry thicket. In a dry channel, where the boulders are covered by moss, I find a curious, striped, white and orange rock. Near this natural curiosity is a disappointingly human artifact — an empty oil jug. Prospectors? Way off in the wilderness — inaccessible, remote and pristine are words that come to mind — a piece of litter, industrial garbage.

Back at camp the three of us share the experiences of our day in the forest. "The elk must already be in the high country," notes Ian. "I might come back in a few weeks and set up a blind along one of the elk trails. Just wait until an elk or a bear comes. The elk are such magnificent animals." Clinton and I admire Ian's patience, imagining him sitting in an elk blind for a week, just waiting.

In the morning we pack up and casually hike down the valley, not in a hurry to leave, photographing the spruce groves and river flats studded with Indian paintbrush along the way. Two deer bound along the river, then up into the woods. Elk tracks are all across the river bar.

From our camp at Power Lake I walk alone into the grove of big Sitkas beyond the lake. The forest floor is damp and open, periodically flooded by the rising lake level. Sword fern glens and salmonberry thickets form a green mosaic amid a maze of sloughs. The giant moldering stumps of a few trees, relics from the hand-logging of fifty years ago, punctuate the

Evening, Brooks Peninsula

the Bunsbys are the slopes of Mount Seaton above Battle Bay, carpeted with ancient forest, part of the jewel in the tarnished crown of Vancouver Island.

A sharp tug on the starter cord brings the outboard back to life. Ian slides the boat backwards from the beach, spins it around, and points the bow south towards the ravaged coast below Mount Paxton. With the salty wind in our faces and ten-thousand kilometres of ocean at our backs, we race among the offshore rocks and islands past the vanquished landscape north of Kyuquot.

DECISION MAKERS

The windowless meeting room of a Campbell River hotel is stuffy and buzzing with nervous tension on this sunny morning. Our friend Tom from Kyuquot invited us to this meeting of the Western Strathcona Local Advisory Council, the group that is planning the fate of the Power River valley. We drove through the night from Fair Harbour to be here, to openly share our experiences in a spirit of co-operation.

The chairman brings the meeting to order and introduces us as representatives from the Western Canada Wilderness Committee * — three swarthy, sunburned explorers just back from the wilds of the Power. Except for Tom and two or three others, the people are cold. A forester from MacMillan Bloedel, whose company has no stake in the area being discussed, says, "Your very presence here is an interference." An interference with what? Your desire to conquer and destroy? I resist the temptation to comment. The tired-looking chief forester from International Forest Products, also without a stake in the Power, leans forward aggressively and suggests that our presence is some pre-conceived evil plot that Tom has orchestrated. I am genuinely surprised. But then his company is responsible for the mess on Mount Paxton and Saint Paul's Dome, and he was upset that *National Geographic* printed a picture of its handiwork.

I wonder how many of these people have even been in the Power valley; have seen the elk tracks in the sand, or have thought about how long fourteen-thousand years of ecosystem development since the ice age is. What we have experienced cannot be shared with closed minds in this hostile atmosphere. We leave.

As we stand in the hallway outside the meeting room, Tom bursts through the door, smiling broadly. "That was wonderful!" he exclaims. "It was just what we needed to show their true colours! I'm so glad you came down." Still smiling, he adds, "So you're on your way now? If you're up in Kyuquot again, do stop by the cove, you're always welcome."

It must be another wonderful day in the Kyuquot wilderness, with clear air and wave-washed sand. The sunshine must be streaming through the spruce forests, casting long shadows on the spongy humus that is home to thousands of unknown and unseen life forms. It seems most presumptuous to think that we understand this ecological treasure enough to perform one more experiment on one more irreplaceable wilderness.

* The author and Mr. Webb are no longer associated with the Western Canada Wilderness Committee.

Southern Chilcotins

MOUNTAINS OF AUTUMN GOLD

I recall seeing a photo of Slim Creek in the Southern Chilcotin Mountains in the 1982 Western Canada Wilderness Calendar. The long valley, blanketed in snow, curved off into the distance, unmarred by civilization. Underneath, the caption read, "This year a logging/mining road will penetrate the Slim Creek Valley." And it did.

The giant slash pile above Slim Creek dwarfs my pickup truck. Tons of waste wood — splintered, broken remnants of 250-year-old lodgepole pine and Engelmann spruce trees — cascade down off the bulldozed landing into a creek gully. The surrounding clearcut is pep-pered with boulders, tombstone-like blocks of pale granite left by retreating glaciers. The logging cut itself is wedged between avalanche chutes. To log such a place, on thin soil far up a mountain valley, seems so desperate. And it is.

Slim Creek is officially part of the Lillooet Timber Supply Area, an area badly over-cut. Too much timber cut too fast. And now the pressure is on the last big pieces of wilderness in the TSA; the Stein Valley and the Southern Chilcotins. With Slim roaded and logged, neighbouring Leckie and Bonanza creeks are next on the block. The wilderness is shrinking.

The Southern Chilcotin wilderness lies in the central and southern Chilcotin Ranges of the Coast Mountains, a transition zone between coastal and interior climate patterns. Not a single hectare of wilderness in this region is protected, despite years of opposition to logging plans, and a number-one priority recreation ranking from the B.C. Parks regional office.

GOLDEN VALLEY

The leaves of the aspen trees are golden in the September sunshine. Fall comes early to the high valleys of the Chilcotin country. Dew dampens the leaves along the trail not yet warmed by the morning sun. Gun Creek, glacial green and turbulent, rushes below, carving its valley a little deeper with each successive, water-carried pebble grating across the streambed like a grain of sandpaper. It is such a wonderful morning in this golden valley, so fresh and clean and full of life. I have always found fall to be too short. That fleeting moment when the colours ripen to their fullest all too quickly passes into the dreary November rains. It is good to know that one can follow the wave of colours across the landscape, from high to low, north to south, for over a month.

The path, heavily worn by horses, curves in and out of aspen groves and pine thickets, between sun and shadow. George Yearsley, John Duffy and I drop our heavy packs in a little meadow and wander down to a bar of water-rounded shale beside Gun Creek. Here we rest for a while in the sun beside the gently burbling creek, contented by thoughts of the days of wilderness exploration that lie ahead. Our hike will form a forty-five kilometre loop, following trails up Gun Creek past Hummingbird and Trigger lakes, over Deer Pass, and down Tyaughton Creek. From Tyaughton, we will crest the pass cradling Spruce Lake, then rejoin the Gun Creek trail.

George — lean, muscular and intense — is truly a connoisseur of wilderness. Passionately attached to the land, vehemently at odds with those who would despoil it, his quest for wilderness has taken him hiking, kayaking and canoeing into remote enclaves throughout the province. I have only known John for a short time, but he has emerged as a reasoned, articulate person, fascinated by nature and culture. As an economist, he is also keenly aware that ecological and economic health are inextricably linked. Our common love for wilderness has brought the three of us together in the flaming autumn hills of the Chilcotin country.

The Gun Creek grasslands are open, west- and south-facing slopes dotted with clumps of

Lodgepole pine

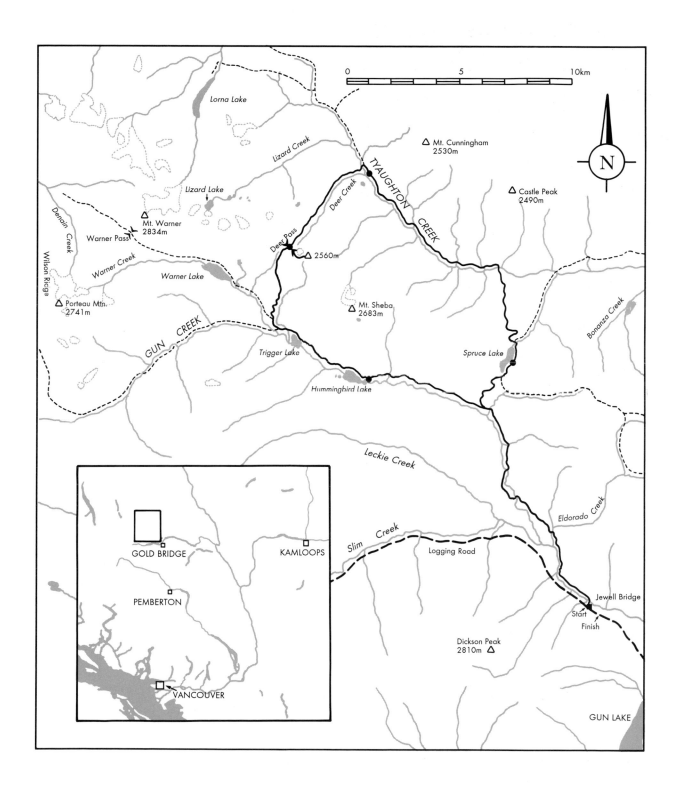

Lorna Lake

Lizard Creek

Lizard Lake

Mt. Warner
2834m

Warner Pass

Denain Creek

Wilson Ridge

Warner Creek

Warner Lake

Porteau Mtn.
2741m

GUN CREEK

Trigger Lake

Deep Pass

2560m

Deer Creek

TYAUGHTON CREEK

Mt. Cunningham
2530m

Castle Peak
2490m

Mt. Sheba
2683m

Spruce Lake

Bonanza Creek

Hummingbird Lake

Leckie Creek

Eldorado Creek

Slim Creek

Logging Road

Jewell Bridge

Start

Finish

Dickson Peak
2810m

GUN LAKE

N

0   5   10km

GOLD BRIDGE

KAMLOOPS

PEMBERTON

VANCOUVER

aspen and willow. The narrow path contours across the valley side, gradually but steadily gaining elevation. On the opposite side of the valley, a northeastern exposure, a mosaic of forest types shows the patterns of past fires and insect infestations that give the natural forest its diversity of habitats. Patches of pale green — younger lodgepole pine stands which regenerated after fires — are intermixed with tracts of dark, pointed Engelmann spruce and subalpine fir. Here and there, groups of old Douglas-fir form tall, craggy islands. The occasional golden aspen grove breaks the green carpet.

The distribution of forest and grassland in the Gun Creek valley is characteristic of the Southern Chilcotin country. The hot, dry microclimate on the south- and west-facing slopes supports grass-

land communities rich in wildflowers, some of them rare. Dense forests cover the cooler, wetter north- and east-facing mountainsides.

Ahead is the high, barren scree of Mount Sheba, originally known as Sheba's Breasts for its twin peaks. We drop into a moist creek gully thick with resin-scented subalpine fir and lodgepole pine, cool and green like an oasis in the tan warmth of the grasslands.

Just past the creek, a simple, weathered pole marks a trail junction. We keep left, up the main valley of Gun Creek towards Hummingbird Lake. The path is vague in places as it traverses grassland slopes and golden aspen groves. In a grove of evergreens near a creek we encounter a weathered log cabin and corral. A hand-lettered sign on the cabin door states:

Empire Valley cow camp cabin

I push open the heavy, creaking door and
am greeted by the damp, musty odour of a shelter inhabited by pack rats and mice. The dark,
claustrophobic interior and dirt floor are not in-
viting — and these aren't "times of Danger."
Outside, the porch is fenced by a collapsing
mosquito mesh wall.

Beyond the cabin, past a horse camp, we
follow the trail as it dips in and out of furrows
in the hillside, winding across meadows and
through aspen and pine groves. This present-
day path closely follows the route of an old
Native hunting and trading trail which traversed
the Chilcotin country from the Bridge River valley to Nemiah Valley near Chilko Lake. Much of
that route still remains wild, offering a precious
glimpse into our cultural history. But that could
easily be lost as logging and mining interests continue to push further into the mountains.

The slopes become steeper, dropping precipitously to Gun Creek where the stream has
undercut its banks. The forest mosaic of the valley spreads out like a wide-angle panoramic
view. Dark, narrow spires of Engelmann spruce
rise out of the valley bottom. Along the trail,
on the warm, dry, south-facing slopes, the
rocky soil supports lodgepole pine and Douglas-
fir. A few ponderosa pines mark the
westernmost distribution of this species in B.C.
Higher on these slopes, the ponderosas are
found in a unique association with whitebark
pine. We crest a shallow ridge near the base of
a rock slide, then descend gently through
sparse pine forest, selecting a pleasant campsite
in the woods beside Hummingbird Lake.

The glacial green water is placid, reflecting
the spires of subalpine fir trees on the shore
and the amber glow in the west. A strong sense

Ancient whitebark pine above Hummingbird Lake

of the wildness of the place pervades. Only
small sounds disturb the stillness — the burble
of fish breaking the surface of the lake and the
more distant rushing of mountain streams. I
dip the cooking pot into the pure water and
watch the ripples glide outwards in concentric
circles. George and John busy themselves setting up the tents and gathering small downed
twigs for a fire. While we conduct tasks inde-
pendently and without structure, they merge
easily into a whole, efficient system, building
the joy of companionship.

SIGNATURES OF ANTIQUITY

Morning brings another calm, clear day.
The milky green waters of Hummingbird Lake

Club lichen on a charred log

reflect intermittent fair weather cumulus clouds gliding overhead.

As John and George continue along the lakeside trail, I climb alone up the talus slopes overlooking Hummingbird Lake to a ridge where ancient weather-beaten whitebark pines cling to boulders crusted with blistered rocktripe, green map lichen and other lichens. One tree has only half its girth covered by living sapwood and bark; the remainder of the trunk is bare, sun-bronzed, resin-rich heartwood weathered by centuries of exposure in the harsh mountain environment. Its limbs, crusted with brilliant yellow wolf lichen, are sculpted into twisting arms holding out irregular clumps of five-needled foliage. The signature of antiquity is written into every aspect of its form.

The trail passes from the open talus slopes into woods permeated with the scent of balsam, then climbs into dry, boulder-strewn clearings on a shallow ridge. Out in the open it is hot and dusty, and our boots raise little clouds from the sun-baked trail surface. Back in the dense forest the path edges the deep gorge of Gun Creek, where the air is cool and the roar of falling water echoes up from the unseen depths. A few minutes later we reach a well-used campsite on the shore of strikingly beautiful Trigger Lake. Ringed by forest and meadows, Trigger's waters are coloured aquamarine by suspended glacial sediment. At its

upstream end is a large meadow, beyond which rise the snow-dappled peaks of Porteau Mountain and Wilson Ridge. North of Warner Pass, 2,834-metre Warner Peak sprawls its grey rock shoulders in the distance. The scene of great beauty seems an appropriate lunch spot, so we settle down on a log by the shore.

Above Trigger Lake, the trail skirts meadows and marshland coloured crimson and gold by the turning leaves of blueberry bushes and low shrubs. Placid backwaters and beaver ponds form a maze of watercourses. Beside a clear creek on the edge of a meadow, a small, fenced pasture surrounds Trigger Cabin, an outfitter's shelter crafted from sun-bronzed logs. Rows of protruding nails and old crosscut saw blades, teeth facing upward, guard the windows against intruding bears. Inside, everything is tidy and well cared for. We rest in the warm pasture by the cabin in anticipation of the long, hot climb towards Deer Pass.

DEER PASS

The trail is steep and dusty with no water close at hand. To either side, the distant splashing of creeks teases us, as we have not filled

A depth and space that is the essence of wilderness

Trigger Lake

our water bottles. Rounded whitebark pines offer only intermittent shade; the three o'clock September sun overhead is still warm enough to draw sweat from our toiling bodies. As the trees begin to thin out, we meet a party on horseback descending from Deer Pass. They are led by Barry Menhinick, a local outfitter who maintains the Trigger Cabin. One of the group has just been thrown from his horse which stands snorting and pawing at the dusty trail. We stand aside to let the other horses pass, exchanging greetings with the riders. Then we skirt widely around the spooked animal and head for the high country.

The landscape soon opens up, with long views up the Gun Creek valley. Sweeping golden meadows dotted with clusters of pines roll up to the barren buff-coloured mountains.

The back side of Mount Sheba emerges from behind an intervening ridge. Late afternoon sun accentuates the contours of the meadowlands, which extend in a succession of rolls and draws around the mountain shoulder towards Deer Pass. A little, spring-fed stream nurtures a garden of wildflowers and moisture-beaded moss pads. Far below, the forks of a braided creek shine silver with reflecting sunlight.

The climb to the pass is a series of precious golden moments, where land and sky assume a vastness, a depth and space that is the fundamental essence of wilderness. This is a place where the richness of time and health and desire for wild places far outweighs material wealth. I am as rich here as any millionaire, with my friends and with all that surrounds me mine to behold for the moment of my passing.

Blustery morning, Deer Pass

Just a few metres below the crest of Deer Pass is a pond and a sheltered hollow perfect for our tents. The sun drops below the saw-tooth horizon of the Coast Mountains, its last rays illuminating the ripples on the surface of the pond. A deep orange glow hovers over the western skyline for a long time, eventually fading to star-studded blue. A cool wind ruffles the tents as we cook dinner in the illuminated circles of our headlamps.

"So what do you think, Stoltmann! Is this incredible, or what?" bellows George enthusiastically, smiling and laughing.

"It's perfect. I don't know why it took me so long to come here."

"It's beautiful, George," adds John as he hunches over the gas stove. "Thanks for suggesting the trip."

Between mouthfuls of soup, George looks up, senses focusing on the stars, the fading western skyline and the capricious breeze flitting through the pass. "Back in the Chilcotins! Yaahh! Right on!" Passionately attached to the land.

The cold bite of fall, a light snow falling, marks the morning. It is remarkable to stand at the crest of Deer Pass and see the change in landscapes from the rugged glaciated peaks of the Pacific Ranges to the south to the sandy, dry, rain shadow Chilcotin Ranges to the north beyond the valley of Tyaughton Creek. There is a very real sense of connection between the coast and interior of a province divided in so many ways by mountain barriers.

After breakfast I climb to the summit of a 2,560-metre peak east of the pass. Gargoyles of reddish rock thrust up from the summit ridge, itself strewn with brilliant red stones. All around are expansive views of valleys and peaks. Here in the heart of the Southern Chilcotin wilderness, the thin ribbon of the Deer Pass trail, our tents and the blue and red specks of George and John on the slopes below are the only signs of civilization. Ravens wheel in the air currents overhead, soaring.

Two hunters on horseback ride through the pass, then traverse around the ridge to the east and out of sight. By mid-afternoon we have packed up our camp and begin the steady descent into Tyaughton Creek valley by way of Deer Creek. The open slopes streaked with the gold of autumn foliage gradually give way to forest clumps and then continuous forest broken only by avalanche chutes. Marmots whistle at our approach, then run and dive into their burrows. In the midst of the forest is a meadow where the trail edges a steep bank above the creek. A final descent through the woods brings us to Tyaughton Creek which courses through streamside meadows and groves of lodgepole pine. A log jam here makes a good crossing, bringing us to several pleasant campsites beside a large pasture. Dropping our packs, George and I dash across the grassy flats and climb a short distance to a rock outcropping overlooking the meadow. John is tired and collapses against his pack for a nap.

TYAX

It is cool, in and out of the sun. From our perch on the outcropping, George and I watch dark clouds moving from the west down Tyaughton Creek valley, known locally as Tyax.

The drab grey curtain of a squall hangs beneath the clouds, dragging across the sombre carpet of spruce and pine.

"Look at John!" grins George, "kicked back against the packs, havin' a snooze. That squall's comin' right through here, buddy! Haaah, hah! That's classic!"

Then the pellets of hail begin, tentatively at first, but soon engulfing us in an intense, white flurry. We take shelter under trees, while John wakes up and grabs his windbreaker. The squall passes quickly, followed by another. The grey veil softens details on the ridges towards Deer Pass to the south, but soon we can see the peaks again. The sun streams through a break in the clouds and meandering Tyaughton Creek shines silver, its rushing filling the valley with gentle music.

Two gun shots pierce the quiet melody. High up on a ridge, where the sun now sits on the horizon line, two horses stand silhouetted. Hunters. The crack of a third shot echoes across the hills.

"That's probably the bullet through the head," remarks George caustically. Something has changed. The innocence and purity of the natural rhythms has been shattered. A deer, or perhaps a bighorn sheep, is dead. I hope that at least they will use the meat; few outdoor pursuits are as disgusting to me as headhunters looking for a trophy to put over their fireplace. It seems to me that it is equally challenging to seek out wildlife and shoot with a camera, placing a portrait of a living creature on the wall.

We walk back across the meadow to our camp, settling down to cook dinner. A warm fire keeps us up late, talking about hunters and ethics and wilderness. Though from different backgrounds, the three of us seem to share a set of unquantifiable values — a feeling, a love for the land, a sense of what constitutes natural balance and the poetry and rhythm of wild places. As the glowing embers fade and I finally zip myself into my sleeping bag, I wonder, Will the concept of wilderness — of land and its community of life left largely undisturbed for its own

The dry Chilcotin Ranges from Deer Pass

sake — and the passions that it fuels, ever be truly understood by those who do not feel its power?

The twenty-first of September brings another sunny morning, crisp and cool with the touch of fall, but quickly warming under the sun's radiance. While John and George finish breaking camp, I sit on the cobbled banks of Tyaughton Creek, absorbed by the serenity, thinking, writing notes.

The path follows the sidehills above the north bank of sparkling Tyaughton Creek, through airy coniferous forest and groves of golden aspens. Occasionally we drop to creekside flats or negotiate eroding scree slopes where the water has washed out the trail. A party of two on horseback passes, an Indian and an older European man headed for a hunting camp in upper Tyaughton Creek. At the last flat, we ford the creek to the start of what George calls the "greasy trail."

The pounding of horses' hooves sometimes turns this trail into a sea of quagmire. At the sight of the first mud hole, George begins to mutter, recalling his previous experience with deep mud here. Picking around the black, horse-trampled quagmire, he shouts in a mock western twang, "Here we go boys! Good ol' greasy trail!" Then he snorts, imitating a horse, and adds jokingly, "Saddle up, boys! Damn horses!" His talk is punctuated by abrupt bursts of dark expletives that seem to convey the depth, viscosity and

Oasis in the dry grasslands

utter blackness of the mud. On this trip we are fortunate, having come after a long period of dry weather, and only a few boggy areas are muddy.

The trail winds up a hillside through dense forest to a dry crest, then traverses a gently sloping plateau. Near an unmarked junction, where the left hand trail angles off towards Spruce Lake, a small pond ringed by boggy meadow reflects the chimney-like spire of Castle Peak away to the north. As we begin to descend towards Spruce Lake, the forest gives way to meadow, and a magnificent sweep of forest and peaks lies spread out before us. The afternoon sunlight etches every tree as an individual spire against a shadow backdrop. Spruce Lake is cradled in a verdant bowl; snow-dusted Dickson Peak rises beyond. We sit for a few minutes, just taking in the view.

The dusty trail switchbacks down to the lake outlet, where private cabins and a forest service campsite are hidden among the trees. It seems too civilized here, so we find an isolated point further down the lake where others have camped before. A beautiful sunset illuminates the lake. The scene inspires a feeling of melancholy; a day from now our time in the wilderness will be over. With tomorrow being the last day of summer, the season is waning in these mountains of autumn gold, and even the clear days cannot extend the daylight hours much past dinnertime.

FULL CIRCLE

Morning brings a dull, drizzly day. The stove hisses under the dense canopy of a spruce tree, bringing the water for our oatmeal and hot chocolate to a boil. A float plane touches down on the lake and taxies over to the little wharf beside our campsite. Two middle-aged couples disembark, carrying travel bags and fishing gear. John talks to the pilot, who explains apologetically that the wind forced him to land at this end of the lake.

Spruce Lake has become a very popular fishing spot, and float planes take off and land frequently enough to impair the feeling of wildness. It would not seem entirely right to ban access to people who come to enjoy the relative solitude, but somewhere a line must be drawn. There is a point, a wilderness threshold, where the level of development or access overpowers the feeling of remoteness. Here at Spruce Lake, the threshold has already been passed.

The path parallels Spruce Lake through the forest for a short distance, then begins to descend into the grasslands above Gun Creek. There are long views down the valley from the switchbacking trail; a tapestry of deep green conifers, golden aspens and beige grasslands is woven between the mountain walls. The weathered post marking the Gun Creek trail junction appears among the tawny grasses and wilted asters. We have come full circle.

Grasslands give way to aspen groves, then to forest. The sweet air smells of rain, but only the slightest hint of drizzle materializes. The forest floor is a quilt of colour with the gold of aspen and birch leaves, maroon of prickly roses, and festive red of bunchberries. Below, Gun Creek rushes loudly among big water-rounded boulders and white-barked aspens. Pines clothe the hillsides, and the cottonwoods drop their mottled yellow leaves into swirling eddies of glacial green. Soon, the peaks will be wrapped in snow and winter will settle upon the landscape.

Walking alone, I have time to reflect on how wilderness has shaped me and become the driving force of my life's ambitions. To express and communicate something of great importance to me gives meaning to my life and work — material wealth is not the basis for satisfac-

Spruce Lake and Dickson Peak

tion. I have found countless hours of happiness walking, skiing, climbing, canoeing or just watching the timeless rhythms of the natural world. I have learned that in a living, dynamic world change is inevitable and leads to renewal and diversification of life and opportunities.

Searching deeper, I recall special wilderness experiences, images that begin to clarify my thoughts, forming links between the physical environment and my emotional connection to it.

The physical power and fury of wilderness has touched me in winds so strong they left me gasping for air, blew my suspended ice axe out horizontally like a fluttering flag, and visibly shook a tin-box alpine hut on its foundations.

Then there are the moments of serenity and grace. Once, sitting alone in a high meadow in the Coast Mountains, scanning the twilight horizon with my telephoto lens, a great, seemingly prehistoric-scale silhouette filled the field of view. Looking up from the camera, the silhouette became a snow-white owl, gliding silently, barely a metre over my head. That experience, like watching a solitary caribou foraging in the high meadows of Tweedsmuir Park, or feeling the black-eyed stare of a northern spotted owl in the ancient

Autumn gold: aspen grove in Tyaughton Creek valley

forest, has brought me closer to the land.

On another occasion, a sense of mystery engulfed me as I emerged from a rain-drenched Vancouver Island forest onto an open Pacific beach long after the sun had set. Soaked and exhausted, I was captivated by the phosphorescent waves crashing on the sand, knowing that as long as there was water in the sea, tides and wind, they would never stop. Later, I began to grasp the almost incomprehensible scale of time at which wilderness functions, as I lay beneath trees that had already lived for over a thousand years when the first Europeans landed on these shores. And beyond the lifespan of the individual trees, the forest was ten times that old.

And watching the sun rise from a mountainside at four thousand metres, I saw the outer limits of our home. To the east, the thin red line of dawn, following the planet's curvature, marked the atmosphere — a fragile, transparent envelope containing and sustaining all life on earth. It became even clearer that what we do within that envelope — our life support system — could influence ongoing patterns of change, perhaps to a degree that will determine if today's species of animals and plants — including humans — will be part of the next phase of this planet. Like an ice age, our actions could set the stage for another phase after which life may evolve anew.

Together with countless others, these experiences represent the power, mystery, time and quiet pulse of the wild. They have clarified my comprehension of our place within the biosphere and the fragility of life. All have

Twilight over the Pacific Ranges from Deer Pass

strengthened my relationship to the land, building a pure, deeply-rooted love for the natural world. And with love comes respect and caring. Just as we care for ourselves and those we love, we must also care for our home — applying a land ethic that sustains not only our own lives, but all life on earth.

The realization that so much of society has lost its affinity with the land brings frightening visions of what the future might hold. But in wilderness is the opportunity to re-kindle a love and respect for the earth and for each other, to re-charge that age-old sense of curiosity and discovery and strengthen our relationship with the land, to chase the human spirit to its very roots.

I cannot expect of others any more than my own modest contribution. Simply leave time to get to know the land and its wonders for yourself. Care for it as you would a loved one. Share the joy of discovery and the thrill of exploration, have fun and laugh. Hike the forests, climb the peaks, ski the icefields, walk the beaches, canoe and kayak the rivers, lakes and seashore. Or just lie in a meadow, breathe the clear air and renew yourself. Stop. Think. Listen. Hear the roaring vastness of a great valley, or the sigh of wind in the treetops, or the eternal thunder of breakers on the shore. Then go back and speak to the world from your heart.

RANDY STOLTMANN is an environmental researcher, writer and photographer who lives in West Vancouver. An avid outdoorsman and environmentalist, he has previously published three books, including *Hiking Guide to the Big Trees of Southwestern B.C.*, and has another in the works. He was a contributing writer/photographer to *Carmanah: Artistic Visions of an Ancient Rainforest.*